EYES HAVE NOT SEEN

THE

TESTIMONIES OF

OUR YES!

THE LAUNCH
C H U R C H

Foreword by Founder
Lee A. Williams, III

EYES HAVE NOT SEEN

THE

TESTIMONIES OF

OUR YES!

Written By: Women of The Launch Church

Compiled By: Pastor Taundra D. Williams

#THEYESMOVEMENT

EYES HAVE NOT SEEN
The Testimonies of our Yes!
#THESYESMOVEMENT

Destiny Speaks International, LLC
PO BOX 1306
Converse, TX 78109
www.Destinyspeaksintl.com

Ordering Information:
Quantity sales. Special discounts are available on quantity purchases by corporations, associations, and others. For details, contact the publisher at the address above.
Orders by U.S. trade bookstores and wholesalers.
Please Attention Big Distribution

Graphic Designer I Krystina D. Cosey I Coseyinnovations.com

Printed in the United States of America

ISBN: 978-1-7349495-0-6

ACKNOWLEDGMENTS

"First, I must thank God for creating me for a purpose greater than my mind could ever imagine. I would also like to thank my family for always believing in me and encouraging me. To my Launch Church family and leaders, Onward from here!"
– *Catherine Elizabeth Garner*

"I first give Glory to my Lord and Savior Jesus Christ for ordering my steps and never giving up on me. I would like to thank my husband James and my son Mike for always supporting me and encouraging me to be my best! I thank my Launch Church family for showing me love and support while reminding me that I can do ALL things through Christ, who gives me strength. Lastly, I must thank my Leaders of The Launch Church Pastors Lee and Taundra Williams for always stretching me to be my best and pulling my purpose out of me to edify God's Kingdom."
- *Lekisha Williams*

"God you are good, and I thank you for loving me, despite me. I would like to thank my three wonderful children for allowing me the room to grow into the mother, teacher, and mentor I've become. You are my strength and purpose to keep pushing past my limits and obtain every goal. Thank you to my Pastors Lee and Taundra Williams for believing in me and properly guiding me to Christ. Thank you to all of my fellow authors, and church family for your support. As my Pastor Lee A. Williams, III said, "This is the year of broken nets.""
- *Jeneea J. Moore*

"I would like to thank God, for giving me the vision and strength to go forward with ministry and writing this chapter of my life. I would like to thank my family for always supporting me in all things."
– *Lisa Spencer-Luke*

"First, I would like to thank The Launch Church, Pastor Will and Pastor Taundra for pushing me into what I am today. I would like to thank my Mother for always being there for me through thick and thin. I cannot forget my sister, my two grandmothers, my other family members and friends. Next, I would like to thank my three boys Melvin, Jaden and Jeremy for giving me life that only a mother would understand, I love you so very much! Lastly, but of the utmost importance, I give God **ALL THE PRAISE** and **THANKS** from the bottom of my heart for creating and molding me for the better."
— *Jasmine Richardson*

"This would not be possible without God's direction. I thank God wholeheartedly for opening the door to this opportunity, my kids for motivating me to be a better me. Finally, I thank God for my Pastors Lee and Taundra Williams, for seeing something in me I didn't see. Thank you for pushing me to greatness. Onward From Here!"
- *Eboni Moore*

"I would like to thank God, my mentor, and the pastors of The Launch Church. This would not be possible if I never would have come and visited. I am so glad I gave God my "Yes". God rescued us all by sending me and my family to the right place at the right time. My life has truly and drastically changed because of Pastors Lee & Taundra Williams."
- *Madlyn Chase*

"I want to thank God, My Creator, for crowning me with wisdom and purpose for my life. To my leaders, parents, and Pastors Lee and Taundra Williams, thank you for ushering me into my destiny. To my daughter, you are the reason I keep going forward, to prepare you for a greater future. Last, but not least, thank you Launch Church family, I love you one and all!"
— *Chiffon D. Turner*

"First, I would like to thank my Lord and Savior Jesus Christ for holding me and guiding me through such a time as this! I want to thank my Mom, for raising me in the church as a little girl and instilling God in me. My Godparents Apostles' TC and Audrey Maxwell for teaching me how to study and stand on God's Word for myself. To My Pastors Lee and Taundra Williams and My Launch Church Family, You guys are simply amazing! Onward From Here!"
– *Tena M. Nalls*

"The journey to my YES has been that of a unique one! God makes no Mistakes and I am confident in knowing that everything I have gone through and experienced has brought me to this unbelievable point! **MY COMPLETE YES!** "
- *Krystina D. Cosey*

FOREWORD

To witness the pen and painted works of My Daughters, biological and spiritual is a very humbling experience. Even as you read the words that I have spent much time examining, my hope is that you will understand the victorious posture of each new author.

This written work is the *"First Jewel"* in the Crown of the many literary works that The Launch Church will produce collectively.

It is also the birthing of a few new amazing authors. Their testimonies will push, position, and posture you for your purpose in their very own individual works. As their Pastor, Pop, Dad, and Covering, I wish to share with the world the joy of my heart, birthed and pushed out by my wife, **"The Destiny Midwife,"** Pastor Taundra D. Williams, For A Tribe of Lionesses.

Daughters of the Launch, **"May You Experience VICTORY!"**

Lee A. Williams, III
Founding Pastor | The Launch Church

PREFACE

Momentum does not happen without a movement. Eyes Have Not Seen - The Testimonies of Our Yes, has been birthed from a place of total surrender. The birthing of The Launch Church by Pastor Lee A. Williams, III, along with Pastor Taundra D. Williams, gained momentum that led to a movement, *A Yes Movement!* As people filled The Launch Church from every walk of life, the question would be asked: *"ARE YOU READY TO TELL GOD YES?"* Testimonies were brought forth and the lives of believers coming alive were witnessed. Pages began to be produced as individuals poured their stories into these chapters. We pray that as you read the testimonies of souled out for Christ people, that their tears, become healing for your soul. May you be provoked to give God your complete **YES** as these women have, who are now living their truth in freedom! Commit to joining. **#THEYESMOVEMENT**

Taundra D. Williams
Pastor | The Launch Church
"The Destiny Midwife"

TABLE OF CONTENTS

INTRODUCTION

Eyes Have Not Seen – The Testimonies of Our Yes is a book compiled of testimonies from women just like you. The Process of a Total Yes to God brings total healing to broken people, it removes rejection for rejected souls and **Catapults** neglected, ostracized, misused, abused and looked over **MISFITS** to their **DESTINY!**

There comes a time in life when you simply hit a brick wall. All you can think about is what you have and haven't done in your life and what your next steps will be. As authors, myself and our spiritual daughters have authentic & relatable stories in the form of testimonies that will let you know you are never alone. Because there is someone else who looks just like you and has experienced the *Freedom of a **COMPLETE YES to GOD!*** Just think...the timing couldn't have come at a better time. My testimony came at a time where I felt lost even though I went to church more than most. How could I, someone who was raised in church, who had never left church, and was a leader in church feel lost? How could a ***First Lady*** feel lost? Even with all the praying, praising, and teaching I did, I hadn't given God my full committed YES! I was instructed to do something by God and because I denied what he told me, and virtually dismissed this part of my life I held up all my resources. This Yes meant I was not in control! It

took me out of my comfort zone, but I was tired of religiosity! One day I felt this tugging to give God more, and to not stop until I knew transformation had taken place. Maybe this is you. Are you searching for God, or to get more from God? A deeper relationship with him? Well get ready for the time of your life. Your Complete **YES to God** will cost you everything and nothing all at the same time. You may lose loved ones, friends, relationships, jobs, material things, wealth, and practically everything you ever cherished. Your Complete Yes to God will be the most painful and power-packed thing you'll ever do! It will also be the most rewarding thing you'll ever say. It will be the most painful and powerful thing you'll ever do. Our Prayer is that you see yourself in one or all these testimonies and decide you need to say **Yes to God!** I challenge you to do it now and do not wait! Right where you are, raise your hands and **Tell God, YES!** Tell him not my Will Lord but your Will be done. **#THEYESMOVEMENT**
I am so proud of each of you!

– Love, Mama T

CATHERINE ELIZABETH GARNER
LEARNING TO TRUST GOD IN EVERY SEASON

Born and raised in the church Catherine Garner has served in almost every capacity within the ministry. Raised and mentored by her parents Pastor Timothy Garner Sr and First Lady Martha Garner. At a young age Catherine has served in many capacities of ministry including usher board, Children's ministry, housekeeping, Hospitality, and Church Administration. Catherine has a heart for people and an eye for detail which is very vital not only in ministry but in life. Catherine is committed to using all her gifts to enhance the Kingdom of God. Catherine is currently working within the ministry as Executive Pastors Assistant. Catherine is an Ambassador for the Single, Saved and Wonderfully Made. As a single woman Catherine is using this season as a platform to Empower others who are struggling to accept Gods timing.

My Testimony

It is my prayer that my testimony encourages anyone who has struggled with loneliness and rejection to consider laying all your burdens down at God's feet and surrender your plans for God's plan by giving Him your complete Yes.

At a very young age, I knew I was different. I didn't seem to fit in with any crowd. I was the opposite of my four older siblings. They were outgoing and had friends, but I was quiet and preferred to stick to myself and read. Don't get me wrong, I wanted to be a part of the in-crowd so badly, but I seemed to be invisible. Invisible, yes that's the best description of how I felt. When I wasn't invisible, I was picked on, so I didn't mind being invisible. Deep down I wanted to be seen and heard but I didn't feel I was good enough for that platform. I had mastered the art of being seen and not heard. This was not something I was told to do, I decided on my own to try and call the least amount of attention to myself as possible. The first memory I had of rejection was at the age of 7. My father, who was in the military, got stationed in El Paso, TX. I loved school and I remember being so excited to meet new friends. On my first day, I realized I was the only African American girl in my class. I wasn't fazed because being a military brat you learned to adapt. It wasn't until recess that kids started to make fun of me. They said my gums were black like my skin and my hair was nappy. Listen, kids can be the coldest! That's when I realized I was different I began to be self-conscious of the way I looked. Around that same time, an adult that I trusted began to verbally and physically abuse me almost every day over several months. I was told I was ugly, that I was dumb, no one would ever love me and many other damaging words that hurt and confused me. First, I had kids at school saying this, now this person I thought was supposed to be an adult and all adults that I knew up to that point were nice and caring. I was devastated and I felt rejected and different. I just wanted to be like everyone else. Age seven was the first time I remember talking and crying to God to make me pretty, make me smart and for people to like me. As I got older, my self-confidence was non-existent. The feeling of not being good enough never went away and I found myself willing to accept any form of attention because it made me feel like I wasn't invisible. I thought I had gotten past that experience and forgave those who hurt me, but the seeds were planted, and the roots ran deep. I didn't understand why I couldn't connect with a lot of people. I started to think back on all the negative words that were said to me and started to echo the words and just badger myself constantly. I wanted true friendships and relationships so badly but it seemed as if it was always out of my reach. I had always wanted that fairy tale life you know, the one that has a bomb career, married, have 2.5 kids, a gorgeous house with a white picket fence all by the sweet age of 30. Sounds great right? Well, as time went on, I noticed the world was moving around me and I seemed to be, yes you guessed it, Invisible and stuck. Folks asking me when I am getting married and having kids as if it is having those elements that prove you've made it to the good life. I wanted those things, but I felt stressed that I didn't have any of it. I noticed people around me flourishing with groups of friends, engagements, marriages with kids, college degrees, great jobs and from the outside looking in, they had the life that I prayed to God for every day. I thought something was wrong with me. I thought I had done everything I could to be a good person and live right. I was in church every time the doors opened, serving in many auxiliaries, I paid my tithes and offerings, but I was still waiting. I was like "okay God I know I'm not perfect, but I am trying," I thought if I did everything right God would give the desires of my heart. I was tired of waiting for the life I thought I wanted. After a while, I started to get discouraged and felt that none of my prayers were being heard by God. I thought that God didn't see me and didn't know who I was. People would come and try to encourage me by saying "Wait on the Lord Cat" or "God has someone for you when you are ready." I honestly wasn't trying to hear all of that. I felt like I had been waiting my whole life (Yes, I was a bit dramatic) and it was time to take control of the situation. I decided to start putting myself out there and making myself available to anyone that seemed interested without consulting God. That led to a lot of unnecessary heartbreak and disappointments because I stepped out of the will of God. The truth is I didn't trust God, and my arrogance to think that I could do life without God is embarrassing. I quickly learned my lesson. Because of my lack of trust in God, I accepted love in any way that I could get it. I just wanted to be relevant to someone. I wasted many years on a few failed relationships and plenty of what we call "situation-ships", that gray area between being friends and couple status. Looking back, I thank God for still protecting and loving me unconditionally despite my selfish, womanish ways. All that time I was still in church like everything was normal, but I was disconnected from God. I was so, wrapped up in what I wanted that I never even sked God what His will for my life was. I wasn't thinking about God's purpose for my life. I was just concerned with being alone. I remember crying to my mom countless times, and she would give me the scripture Proverbs 3:5,6 *"Trust in the Lord with all thine heart and lean not unto thine own understanding. In all thy ways acknowledge him, and he shall direct thy paths."* I would just roll my eyes and say, yes ma'am. My mom seemed to have a scripture for every issue I came to her with. In my mind I thought she doesn't understand, I'm doing all of that and not seeing any clearer, but that scripture has always stuck with me. At the age of 30, I was told I would most likely not be able to have children and I thought that was the end for me. That devastated me more than anyone knew. I was not sure at that point in life if I even wanted children and when the option is taken away its difficult to accept. In my mind I thought Cat you are still single and you may not be able to give a man a child if you ever do get married, what do you have to offer? I put on a brave face to everyone, but I felt so empty. I became an expert at smiling and being happy in public and going home wanting to die. I have always been the strong one for everyone else and had no strength for me. I felt like I had no purpose in this life I remember crying myself to sleep so many times asking God not to wake me up. I felt hopeless, worthless and lost with no purpose. Eventually, God stripped my life of everything I found comfort in. My job, my church and the few friends I thought that I had. I felt alone and completely vulnerable. At my lowest moment with all the strength I had, I asked God to save me because I felt myself getting further away from Him than I've ever been. I told God I didn't want to die. One night I attended what I thought was an Open House for a new ministry The Launch Church just to support, or so I thought. While I was there, I heard God clearer than I ever have in my life. God asked, 'Do you trust me?' I told God I was scared but I trusted Him. He told me to commit. In my mind, I was thinking this is absolutely nuts. I am a natural born planner and over-thinker, so this decision was out of character for me, but I trusted God because after everything He was still there for me. On that night I gave God my first yes and committed to The Launch Church. After I committed, I said to myself I'm not going to serve in any capacity because I just need to work on me. God said no ma'am you have the heart to serve. I found myself saying yes to everything with joy in my heart and I was at church every time the doors opened. With every yes, I noticed my heart's focus began to change. While attending one of our services the question was posed, Will you give God your Complete Yes? That question echoed so loudly in my ears I couldn't hear anything else. God was asking me to surrender my will to Him. I felt like I was the only person there that night I didn't walk I ran to the altar and surrendered my will to God. I knew God was speaking to me. I knew this could be my last chance to get my life back on track for real. I told God I have nothing else to lose and I am all in and for the first time, I completely let go I knew I couldn't live the way I have been living and I couldn't continue to do things my way because I was messing things up. I was so exhausted from trying to navigate to a life I thought I wanted, I needed a change. It was very hard for me to utter that first 'Yes, but as soon as the words crossed my lips, I immediately felt God's arms wrap around me. The feeling was unlike any other. The love and acceptance I had been seeking all this time I finally had and I had always had it through Christ. An overwhelming joy and excitement about my future came over me. Right at that very moment, I said, God, I want to start fresh. I put my past present and future in your hands. I am so thankful for my Pastors, their Yes saved my life and my Yes has changed my life. After I said yes to God, I noticed that my focus shifted from pursuing what I wanted from life to pursuing God's purpose for my life. God has been peeling back the layers of my past like an onion blossom. I've had to face a lot of things I wanted to just ignore. I was still holding on to hurt and pain which was preventing me from moving forward. One day while praying, I asked God how I got to the point that I was so desperate to be accepted. God immediately brought me back to when I was that little 7-year-old girl After all the years that had gone by, I never thought what happened then would affect me at 37 years old. I asked God to free me from the pain, disappointment, low self-image, regret and I released all of it to Him. After surrendering to the process. I am finding myself stepping out of the shadows. I am being stretched and pushed into my purpose. I have never been a public speaker, but I told God I am ready to be used however, He wanted to use me. I thank God for my church family and leaders because every day they encourage me to go beyond my comfort zone. I know now that my season of Singleness is for a purpose and I believe that purpose is to encourage others who may feel discouraged and are struggling within this season. I am still single but I'm learning that in this season I can take my time to find out who I am in Christ. God is behind the wheel and I am enjoying the ride. I had to ask God for forgiveness because I had been trying to fit in not realizing all the while that He created us to stand out. God has granted us the grace and mercy to hit that reset button and pursue our purpose through Him. One of my favorite scriptures that I read daily is Jeremiah 29:11 *"For I know the plans I have for you, declares the Lord, plans to prosper you, plans to give you hope and a future."* I don't know what God has planned for me, but I am ready. My new focus is God's will for my life. I know at times life can make you feel alone, hopeless and lost, but in your lowest moment, you must remember God is right there with you. He wants us to cast all our cares upon Him. God knows all and sees all, but He still wants us to come to Him and bring Him all the things that burden us. God knows Reach one of us by name. He knows each follicle on our head, he knows everything we say and don't say. He

20

wants us to trust and depend on Him. It is not too late to hit the reset button surrender to God and just say Yes to His will. Say Yes today and your life will never be the same! I pray that God keeps and strengthens you in this season.

LEKISHA N. WILLIAMS

FROM BROKENNESS TO BLESSINGS

I was introduced to church at an early age. Born and raised in Adkins Texas, currently reside in San Antonio Texas. I am a worshipping woman of God who loves reading and studying God's word, teaching and encouraging men, women and children to give their life to Christ and follow his example. I have a passion for teaching and encouraging others of all ages and backgrounds, my heart especially goes out to youth and young adults. I have an uncomplicated teaching style that simply breaks down the word of God so that anyone can understand it and apply it to their everyday life. I have served in several Ministry positions including the Sunshine Ministry that reaches out and encourages sick, shut in and bereaved members as well as celebrating their birthdays anniversaries and more. I also have served in the Outreach, youth, Hospitality and greeters Ministries. I am forever grateful to Senior Pastor Lee A Williams for giving me my first teaching job. Teaching the women's group steadfast sisters at Wheatley Heights First Baptist Church. where I encouraged women from different walks of life to quiet the distractions of the world so that they could sit at Jesus's feet and develop an intimate relationship with him. In 2019 I rededicated my life to Christ through the launch Church ministry with pastors Lee Williams, III and Pastor Tandra D. Williams. Where I am fortunate enough to be the youth director. As well as a member of the five-fold ministry leadership group. I am a speaker, an Intercessor and a published author featured in the book "Eyes have not seen."   (Pastor Taundra D. Williams and Lee Williams, III of The Launch Church). I currently continue to take courses and study in the areas of Youth counseling, writing and editing. I am a proud wife to my wonderful husband James Williams Since February 2013, and a mother to our awesome son Michael. God has blessed me farther than I could have ever imagined. I continually trust Him to order my steps and guide me into becoming all that he has called me to be.

My Testimony

Life might not always work out the way that you've planned it. However, no matter what you've gone through, hold on to your faith, put your trust in God, and allow Him to order your steps. Please let me share my journey with you about how I have had to overcome obstacles, leading me to give God my complete yes.

After reading this story, I hope that you learn how to push through obstacles, overcome brokenness that will help you to grow your faith encouraging you to give God your complete Yes, and prepare you to receive all of the blessings that He has in store for you.

I was a happy child, but life experiences caused my happiness to diminish. From a young age, I struggled with being rejected, my mother loved me the best that she could, but she was just a child at the age of 16. I lived with her off and on but mostly lived with my grandparents. I understand that my mother may have been still trying to find herself, but as a child, I felt alone and rejected as if no one loved or cared for me. My grandparents were there, but they were older and reserved. My mother was still in my life. She provided for me financially and visited off and on. Still, when she left, I felt abandoned, and deep down inside, I just wanted my mommy. At the age of 21, most young adults would probably be excited to reach this milestone of adulthood, but I was devastated because my mother passed away at an early age of just 37. By this time, I had lost my grandmother, my mother, and not too long after my grandfather. I was a young adult and had already experienced so

25

many losses that I felt I was not supposed to be happy. I kept my problems to myself, hoping they would just go away. I would put on a fake smile and act like everything was okay. I felt like dying inside. I was secretly screaming for help and on the verge of having a nervous breakdown. I taught myself to suppress my feelings because, over the years, I got used to being talked about by the people close to me. When I reached out to others for help instead of getting help, they made me feel worse. I learned to keep things to myself and not deal with them. For some reason, I lied to myself, making myself think that if I tucked my feelings away, they would just disappear. However, that is not what happened. The problems would make me bitter, sick with high blood pressure, and trigger me to be emotional at times. It was easier to pretend that everything was okay. Once again, I felt alone and abandoned like no one cared about what was bothering me. On the outside, I wanted everyone to think I was fine, but on the inside, I needed someone to hold me tight and let me know that everything was going to be okay. The world taught me that I was unworthy and undeserving of love. I had carried a lot of brokenness from my childhood over to my adult life. I attended church, but it wasn't helping me with the feelings that I had. What is the point of attending church if there aren't any changes? I assumed that I would find love and support at church, but there was a time where I only felt more abandoned, more alone, more judged than ever. I needed love, I needed help, but I didn't know who I could trust or where I could turn. When you're in a pit or dark place, you're thinking becomes cloudy, and you can't logically comprehend the right things to do. I was headed down a path of destruction and was a very broken person. Just when I thought things couldn't get any worse, they did. It was the day before Easter Sunday. My family and I had planned on going to Easter service the next day. I didn't have a vehicle at the time, so I took the bus and was having some "me time" getting my hair and nails done for church service. When done, I decided to stop and get something to eat at a restaurant across the street from where I lived. I took my food to go. I was walking across the street. I remember getting halfway across the crosswalk when from my right side, I was hit by a car! My eyes were still open, and I remember being up in the air spiraling. I lost consciousness at some point because when I was first hit, there was still daylight outside, then I remember waking up in the dark. I was lying on my back in the street during heavy traffic. At this time, there were people gathered on each side of the streets watching me in disbelief. My first thought was to hurry and get up because I didn't want to get hit by another car. When I went to get up, I was in a lot of pain and could not move. I remember thinking my worst fear is if I die here, I will never see my family and friends again, and they won't even know what happened. I needed to call someone and let them know what's going on. I always say that the old me did die that day because it opened my eyes to see how precious life is and what is most important. From the accident, I later found out I had a torn rotator cuff, a broken leg, a gash in my right thigh with a hematoma, two herniated discs, and would even later develop a blood clot in my lung that was life-threatening. I was now mentally and physically broken. While recovering, some old feelings that I had suppressed started to resurface. On top of that, the car accident had me suffering from depression, anxiety, fear, just to name a few. It was one of the hardest things that I have ever had to endure. I had a lot of love and support, but deep down inside, I still felt alone and abandoned like there was no one that I could talk to. I have had many sleepless nights and now not only dealing with internal pain I was now struggling with physical pain. I was lower than I had ever been. This is the moment that I felt like I had nowhere else to turn except to God. I gave my life to the Lord, and although I had been in church, I realized I hadn't fully given myself completely to the Lord. Instead of me trying to control everything, I said: "Lord, I have tried to control my life and failed horribly, so now let's try this again but with you." I started getting back into church regularly. I started praying more. When I felt alone and abandoned, I would read scripture and study God's word. I dedicated most of my time to church, getting involved with as many auxiliaries as possible. I started to get serious about walking with the Lord. I felt like I was on the right track. However, I would eventually find that I was still broken and still needed help. I quickly realized that it doesn't matter how many organizations that you serve on at church that will determine if you make it to Heaven. God is concerned about the posture of your heart, and my heart was still bitter and broken. Instead of getting healed, I just got more tired and more frustrated. I was ready to give up on life, I was ready to give up on myself, and I was ready to give up on church. I was stuck in a pit deeper than ever. For many years I allowed fear, rejection, timidity, and anger, just to name a few, control me. I regret that I have allowed these things to make me miss out on many opportunities because I was too afraid to pursue them. Since then, I have learned to walk in confidence because God has not given us the spirit of fear, but of power and of love and of a sound mind (2 Timothy 1:7 NKJV BibleGateway. I can do all things through Christ who strengthens me (Philippians 4:13 NKJV BibleGateway). Giving God my complete Yes was the best thing that I have ever done. My life has completely changed for the better. I have learned to forgive the people that have done me wrong. We cannot expect God to forgive us if we do not forgive others. Now I have a positive outlook on life. I put more time and energy into my purpose and doing the things that God has called me to do. God loves you so much that He will not leave you in a dark pit or a broken place. He wants the best for your life and welcomes you with open arms. By giving God my complete Yes with Him, I have overcome many obstacles, now headed down the right path and experiencing a better life like never before. I am not saying that I no longer have obstacles, but with the Peace of the Lord, my Outlook is different. I know that I will make it through tough times because He will never leave me alone, and I have Him fighting with me. Even though I was in a dark place, I continued to read and study God's word, but I isolated myself and took a step back from church. I was done, and I asked God what was next for my life. Soon after, I would find out that my youth pastor from my current church was starting a new church called "The Launch Church." That is the type of God I serve!! As soon as I felt like I couldn't go on, He stepped in and gave me a way out! When I was weak, He was strong!! I Praise God because I felt like as soon as I was ready to throw in the towel. God came to my rescue. Ever since I have joined The Launch Church, I have been going through a process of deliverance that I have never experienced before in my entire life. The leaders' Apostle Lee Williams and Pastor Taundra Williams are so loving and caring. They are always willing to do whatever it takes to help you to become all that God has called you to be. The Launch Church is not just another church that's focused on religious practices and getting another member to keep a pew warm. They are focused on deliverance, setting healthy and redeemed people free from what is keeping them from their God-given purpose. They not only help you to discover what your purpose is in life, but they give you the tools to learn how to use your gifts. Then they support and encourage your growth to set you free into the world to serve in the area that God has called you to. With the help of The Launch Church's God lead leaders. For the first time, I realized that there was a legitimate reason why I felt the way that I did. They helped me to pinpoint the root cause of many problems that I faced. With their help determining the root cause of some of my issues, it has helped me begin the process of healing. They are helping me mend my broken heart. I ask the Lord daily to create in me a pure heart and to renew the right Spirit Within Me (referenced Psalm 51:10 NIV) As I go through the process of deliverance. All the hurt and the pain from my past does not affect me. I now know that I have love and support, and now I am not fighting alone. I have God and individuals who genuinely love and care for me. Although I still have work to do. I feel free from bondage and am finally on the path to healing. I am working on myself and becoming all that God has called me to be. We may not be able to help some of the things that have happened to us in the past. We might not be able to change some of the bad decisions that we have made. We can, however, ask God for forgiveness and invite Him into our hearts. He will put the right people in our paths to help us to heal, be delivered, and walk into our purpose that God has created for each of us. We each have a purpose in life, and we were not solely created just to work ourselves to death or to be poor and live broken. The Lord promises to give us hope and a future, He has a plan for our lives (Jeremiah 29:11 NIV) to give us a life and have it more abundantly (John 10:10 NIV) (referenced for scriptures but paraphrasing). We must resolve the issues of our hearts. I am finally putting my trust in God because He has never left me nor forsaken me. (Deuteronomy 31:6 NIV). Each of us needs to be healed and delivered so that we will not be the cause of someone else's hurt, pain, or brokenness. I lived as a broken person for a very long time, but God loves me so much that He did not leave me in my brokenness. When I came to the point in life where I got tired of being broken and living with hurt and pain. I made the decision that I deserve better. I finally realized that God also wanted a better life for me. He was politely waiting on me as a gentleman would. It is never too late to start again with the Lord because He loves you and is waiting for you. He was with me and is with me every step of the way, even when I didn't realize it. I am keeping my eyes focused on the Lord and allowing Him to order my steps. Since giving God my complete yes and trusting Him with my life. I have gone from brokenness to blessings, and all the glory goes to God. I thank Him for the people that He has put into my life to help restore my heart. No matter what it is that you have been through when you truly give your heart over to the Lord, He will heal you. The Launch Church has helped me to discover what my purpose is in life. They are teaching me how to use my spiritual gifts, which I now realize I have had all along. My hurt, pain, distractions, fear, and depression has kept me from realizing that God chose me for a reason. I am now learning that confidence is my portion, and I am the daughter of the King of kings. I am beautiful and loved; I may have made some mistakes, had failures and disappointments, but God has not given up on me. God has not given up on you! He wants you to give Him your heart and to develop an intimate relationship with Him. Allow Him to deliver you and set you free from all the distractions that keep you bound and holds you captive. I recommend that you walk by faith and not by sight, hold on to God's unchanging hand with faith as big as a mustard seed. Don't look back to issues of the past but look forward to a new or renewed life with Christ! He sent out His word and healed them; He rescued them from the grave. (Psalm 107:20 NIV)

JENEEA J. MOORE

TRANSFORM MY LIFE

Jeneea J. Moore CEO of JC MOORE INTERNATIONAL LLC and Saved Over Success was born and raised in Chicago, Illinois. She was raised in a broken home but learned not to allow that broken to be her ending story. After the birth of her wonderful young sons, she decided to change her life, for them. Charles, Cobe, and Jamin Moore are her fuel and passion to demolish limitation and obtain all of her goals. She learned how to annihilate generational curses, break soul ties, and overcome disabilities that will lead her to the completion of her Master's Degree in Business Management. The Moore family became proud members of The Launch Church-SA under the leadership and Founder Pastor Lee A. Williams III and Taundra Williams. The Moore family has a strong belief in God, Jesus Christ, and the Holy Spirit. They're saying is, "We're better together, but Greater in God!

Ms. Moore is a motivational, informational and transitional speaker. Her goal is to help transition people from their pain and resentment to their full purpose. She is currently studying to become a transitional life coach, building the Saved Over Success Network and Moore Production company were her next series of books will be published.

Amongst her soon to be new business endeavors, we don't see her stopping anytime soon. From spreading the word of God, speaking engagements, managing others business, promoting brands, event planning, rapper, singer, author, poet, and friend...Jeneea Moore's job is never done.

She's been remembered mostly for her Face book Live T.V. Shows. Jeneea J. Moore has ministered at several events like The House of Prayer, "Woman of Excellence in Red", Vosa Youth G.A.N.G "Mid-Summer Youth Bash" "The Broken Woman Ministry", "The Women's Pillow Conference", Dream Week, "Creating Our Vision", and Dr. Lulu's "Parenting Your Teen Workshop". Radio personality on "KROV FM Radio", "KCHL Gospel 1480", Talk Show host on "Tha1 Media" and Saved Over Success Network. ". She covered media for Kingdom Legacy Records "Red Carpet VIP Gala", Brenda Kay, "Artist Night Out Exhibit" while creating her events on the Saved Over Success events like "Woman's Concert", "Poetry Brunch" and many more. Jeneea J. Moore knows how to light up the room with her personality, joy, peace, and sense of humor and hopes to bring that say joy to others.

My Testimony

Dearly Beloved,

I write to you today, in hopes this letter reaches you in time. We're living in a world where there's a constant threat against our lives. Christianity has conformed in many ways to fit this new world era of believers. The term "church hurt" has become an anthem used by believers to bring about the destruction of one's self. We're fighting against ourselves instead of groaning in the spirit or conquering the principalities that's trying to thwart our very being. Every moment of the day we're warring between our past failures and our future success.

We constantly fight against ourselves, with the continued mind play and bewildered torches of our deepest fears and darkest regrets, tormenting our inner man with failures, let-downs, and defeats. We must change the trajectory of our minds. We must seek God within our spirit, heart and soul by leaving our past behind us and breaking all barriers and generational curses. Annihilating every limitation put on us by people. You must understand failure is not an option. Why? It is vital to the many unanswered prayers from those attached to you, for you to gain the spiritual freedom that comes from you, YES! Do you realize your YES is connected to hundreds of believers, breakthroughs? There are women waiting on your words of encouragement. They're waiting on your ministry to reach their lives. They need your YES.

Hear me, for I come to you in peace. I come to you with the love of God. I come to you with clarity and strength to help you carry and bear your own cross. You may feel burdened down; you may even have moments of loneliness and fear of discomfiture. Now I will be the first to say, I've experienced the deception that comes from the pit of hell. I've been lost and confused. I've been lied to and made to believe that I didn't have a purpose.

But, let me reassure you, this is your day of redemption. This is the day of restitution. From this day forward, and by reading the testimonies within this book, you will gain the necessary tools to obtain your own personal breakthrough. Listen, we want you to win. We want to celebrate the manifestation of the Lord with you. Through our testimonies, you'll gain an understanding of why your YES is so important. **YOUR YES MATTERS!** Let me tell you why...

Not long ago, I was in a spiritual environment that almost killed me. Literally, I was dying inside and almost didn't notice it until it was too late. The structure of ABC church was very toxic, manipulative, and controlling. A military base is what I called it. Generally speaking, in the military, you have your Privates, Staff Sergeants, Captains and other ranking officers. Now in any branch of the military, the commanding officer gives out orders. No one speaks, sleep or even uses the bathroom without what I call, "Prior Authorization." In the military, most soldiers can't even think for themselves without direct orders from their superior officer. This is what one will call, Spiritual Control or manipulation or even witchcraft. But I call it "Major Deception."

ABC church was structured just like that. I couldn't even make a sensible decision without consulting my pastor first. We were trained to follow orders. A simple thing like putting in a job application was discussed, what to wear, what and when you could speak to people in the church, which included your own family. Heck, we couldn't even fellowship with church members outside of the church. Imagine if you couldn't socialize with members within the church; visualize how bad we were ridiculed for fellowshipping with believers who attended other ministries.

Now I get it, you can't eat off every plate and you shouldn't go to every service. But there is a problem when you're not allowed to visit another church's ministry, ever. Everyone isn't out to steal your members. There are some great men and women of God, whose divine calling is to travel the world, spreading the Gospel of Christ. We can only pray that we're under a ministry that has all five folds within the church. But let's be honest, every church barely has an Apostle or Prophet, let alone an Evangelist or Teacher in house. If you aren't allowed to gain what you need outside of the house to better your spiritual growth or servitude inside the house...It's called CONTROL.

I recall that time when I bought a ticket for my first ever Women's Conference, at what I believed to be a family church. I'd known this pastor for years; I met him through my current pastor at the time, so why would this be a bad idea? I went to Thursday night's service to ensure it wasn't on a day that we had service, so I wouldn't receive any back lash.

Dr. Matthew Stevenson, III was the speaker of the night. Look, when I tell you, I was the loudest person in the room. The place was packed; I had to sit in the back of the room in the overflow section. By the time Dr. Stevenson was done with his message, I had to create an altar right at my seat. Snot was running out of my nose so bad that I had to breathe out of my mouth. Ask me if I care, nope! (Thank God someone brought me some tissues, though.) All I knew, I needed a change. I had to separate myself from the people I was dealing with, relationships and spiritual bondage. I knew from that very moment; I no longer wanted to be treated like I was nothing, scum, or lesser than, I knew God had something greater for me, but how will I get there?

As soon as I walked out of the door headed home, I received a call from Pastor Derks; I guess someone told him I was there. He talked about me like I was a foolish dwarf woman. He even talked about the Pastor of the church and Dr. Stevenson like they were wolves in sheep's clothes. I didn't know what to say. Normally when he was on his rant, we didn't say anything at all. I endured one of the worst yelling, belittling, downgraded, verbal condemnations I would receive from Pastor Derks that day. I remember being so devastated and confused at the same time. Everything that I just received from Dr. Stevenson, my breakthrough, my deliverance, my clarity was destroyed in minutes.

In January, God began to speak mightily to me about my future. The first time, God specifically told me to answer the call of Ministry. Understand, we weren't taught that women could preach. Therefore, I had to prepare myself for rejection after informing pastor Derks that I am an Evangelist. He didn't take it well in hidden fear that one of his most faithful members would leave one day. He began to choose his words very carefully, making sure not to tell me that I was mistaken and that wasn't the assignment over my life. I dramatically began to cry. I didn't know what to do with the information; I only knew it was my responsibility to answer the call, but Pastor Derks responsibility to prepare me for my calling. We ended the conversation with no plans of me attending school or being trained in ministry. I was simply told to wait.

Like clockwork, each year beginning in January, God would unction me to preach the word of the Lord. And every year, Pastor Derks would find some reason for me not to begin training. My prayer to God was to be real; I mean really real. Transform my life, Lord, to be amongst the greatest. I mean Dr. Juanita Bynum real, or Dr. Cindy Trimm, real. Apostle John Eckhardt, type of real. Better yet, Pastor Lee and Pastor Taundra Williams real.

When I speak to the Lord, I ask for the Fire of God to speak through me. I need to be above reproach, blameless, spiritually mature. In other words, I need your Glory!

January 2019, God spoke to me again, He told me specifically, YOU NEED TO BE TAUGHT! I didn't know what that meant, nor did I dare to ask God about His plans He had for me. But God kept repeating those very words; YOU NEED TO BE TAUGHT! I knew I needed to tell Pastor Derks what the Lord said, although I know he would question if it was really God talking to me.

Once I told him that God said, "I need to be taught," he stated he wasn't going to teach me ministry and if I wanted to leave, then go. "I'm not in the place to teach or ordain a woman in ministry," although he obtained his Doctorate in Theology. What he meant was he wasn't going to train a woman to preach or evangelize. I just broke down and cried. The church I have known over a decade will not help me reach my next level in God or ministry. I continued to seek God in my private time; communing with Elohim is everything. It's in your private time when you gain clarification on your purpose. In your private time is when you'll receive instructions to whom you should follow and how you can build a closer relationship with the Holy Spirit.

A couple of months later, I finally left my home church; I could no longer be disobedient to the instructions of God. Those few words, "YOU NEED TO BE TAUGHT" would continue to weigh heavily upon me. I couldn't shake it. But I knew I had to go because I was dying inside. I was horrified to leave and walk on faith without the covenant of a spiritual leader. But I've given God my YES. I told the lord He had to place me where He needed me to be where I could gain the proper teaching. Where me and my children could be loved and protected. I had to trust God in this process...like never before. Your YES requires submission and Commission. Your YES requires complete trust in God's process. Your YES tells God you are completely open to whatever He decides to do for or with your life. Your YES MATTERS!

I began trusting God in ways that I've never had before. I began attending service under another leadership, which was going well when in walks Pastor Lee Williams III, and Pastor Taundra Williams for our 9am Leadership training class. I remember like it was yesterday. Pastor Lee began preaching on the very issues I asked God to deliver me from. Every word pierced my soul. The entire church was on fire, and so was I. I was sitting behind the camera recording the church service when Pastor Lee began shouting, "the devil wants to sift you as wheat." God began to physically shake my hand to back and forth, visually demonstrating how someone was sifting wheat.

After shaking my hand back and forth about three times, I jumped up and started shouting. In that hand motion, the spirit of the Lord told me, this is what the enemy is trying to do, destroy life. I went from jumping up and down to lying prostrate on the floor. I wanted to be changed for all of my iniquities. And that day, I gave God another YES!

I began following Pastor Lee shortly after that encounter. I told Pastor Taundra that I'm supposed to be under Pastor Lee Williams, III leadership because there are something's he has to teach me. This conversation occurred before TLC was created. I was so excited, I'd found my teacher. Because I gave God my YES, He placed me in the right place at His appointed time to connect with the man and woman of God that were designed to take me to my next level in Christ.

I knew Pastor Lee was my ordained Pastor, but I had no idea what that process would entail. After the official opening of the Launch church, I began a series of deliverances. No, I mean a series. I had many forms of demonic influences, and I wanted them all gone. You may not understand what I am saying, but I needed to be released from generational curses. I needed to be delivered from spiritual molestation. I needed to be set free from these strongholds that have been keeping me in bondage for many years. I needed to be delivered from any spiritual immortality, negative thought, demonic eggs or seeds planted unknowingly. I wanted to be free.

I have experienced mistreatment from family members and so-called friends. I've been in abusive relationships way more than I can count. I've been spiritually abused, talked about because of my past for way too long. I no longer wanted people to look at me and see my sins. The worst thing some Christians do is treat you according to what they think your sins are or the demons you must fight.

Because of my YES, I connected with God in ways you couldn't even imagine. I learned how to cry out to Him for myself. I learned and received the evidence of speaking in tongues. I learned how to submerge myself in His world. I learned how to build my spiritual man in order to release those unauthorized guests that negatively affected my life. I learned how to forgive the "The Major Deception," that I talked about in my upcoming book. I am no longer that young, foolish woman everyone tried to convince me to be. I am a daughter of the Most High God. I'm Free, no longer captive to the enemy. And it all began with a YES!!!

LISA SPENCER- LUKE

WALKING INTO MY CALLING

Lisa Luke attended church as a child and accepted Jesus Christ as her Savior at the age of 9 years old. Though an adolescent she received her talents and gifts from God. Her first teachers in leadership were her Father and Mother. She began to learn about the gift of prophesy her talents in music and art progressed. Lisa was a member of youth choir/adult choir praise team.

Lisa was called to preach in her young adult life. With her continued education in Ministry she was license and ordained as an Evangelist/Ministry. She held position in the church as Administrative assistant, Finance clerk, Youth Minister, Overseer of Youth Praise Team and currently part of ministry group of intercessors and praise team.

Lisa is currently continuing her Education in prophecy, intercessory Prayer. She is currently married to a God-fearing Man Bobby Luke and is enjoying her life with her children, Jalisa, Leslie, Jessica and Jasmine. Her pride and joy are her three grandchildren Arianna, Jerimiah and Josiah. Lisa Lives her life for Christ! Onward from here!

My Testimony

My goal is to encourage believers to walk in their calling.

At an early age, I knew that I would be walking in my calling. My siblings and I were raised in the Church. Their teaching help set the path God wanted us to take. The Ministers rejected me because I was not traditional. I finally joined a church that would train me. I realized I was taught in religious ways, not according to the gifts Gods given me. I was set back spiritually and not adequately prepared. I began to doubt my ability to minister and walk into my calling. I was dealing with some church hurts and rejection. The pain and rejection I felt made me feel unworthy of God. Staying in my place was taught to me. Someone told me I do not have the anointing of ministry, and I was too young to minister, and women don't preach. I was assigned the jobs to do backstage work, while other Ministers who could speak well served. I was talked about amongst Pastors and told not to expect me in their ministry. Spreading throughout them was rumors and gossip about me. Because I was soft-spoken and did not whoop and holler, I was labeled unworthy. There were only a few who see what God saw in me. It took me a while to find what path to follow in ministry. After prayer, God led me to The Launch Church.

The Pastors of the Launch church ask me if I wanted to be a part of their Church. They explained to me The Launch Church Purpose and Vision. I was so excited. The first service I attended, I joined. The Launch Church is led by two Pastors who are down to earth and God-fearing people who understand my purpose in the ministry.

Because of my past hurts, I had low self-esteem. I was shy and thought I was a disappointment to God. The Leaders of the Church were patient with me and encouraged me according to the Word of God.

Attending service, I realized that the Launch Church was not your traditional Church. Spoken was the word of God. Prayers offered; there were deliverance and healing at every service. There is an auxiliary for every age group and great fellowship amongst our members. Members celebrate each other accomplishments. The Launch Church is a peaceful organization where there is room to grow spiritually. Members have been healed of their infirmities and set free. Taught at every service is the Word of God. I did not realize how much pain I was carrying around in my heart. Once delivered, my life changed; my appearance even changed. The Launch Church is a judgement free zone. I experience deliverance, from several things, mostly hurt. My gifts were needed, and I know God loves me.

I gained confidence in myself. I was ready to work in the Church. I began to sing in the choir. Singing was my way of crying out to the Lord. When I sung, I was set free of things holding me back. I was accepted in a group within the church leaders' group best things that happen to me. I was in a class with people who had the same gifts I had. No one thought of me as weird. They excepted me as a prophetess and a seer.

The Launch Church excepted me for who I am. Immediately I was trained in my gifts. I have learned how to pray and defeat demons. I have learned, as my gifts heighten, how to encourage my brothers and sisters in Christ and support them on their journey. I have learned to do God's will. God has given me a prayer language speaking in tongues and to heal and deliver in prayer.

God has given me the confidence to minister freely according to his will. Since joining the Launch Church, I have moved on from singing on to the Praise Team to Praise Dance/Flag Ministry and fighting Demons in Prayer. The Launch Church has allowed me to be who I am entirely in ministry. There is no judging, only training, deliverance, the word, God's anointing, and freedom. I am who God says I am. I am Victory, walking in my calling. No one can label me as unworthy or put anyone else before me. I don't have the spirit of fear; I am bold For Christ. I am not afraid to stand up for Christ. I am not afraid to speak his word.

At the Launch Church, I was able to see clearly what my mission and purpose was. I was an emotional train wreck. I was depressed and felt worthless to God. As I listen to teachings from Pastor Lee Williams and Pastor Taundra William, I felt my worth. I began to feel better about myself. I felt like I was a soldier in God's army, and I am important. God has chosen me at this time to help set people free and of spiritual death. God led me to encourage and put a smile on people's faces. I was teaching them that God does love everyone, even sinners. I've learned prayer changes things. My husband, Bobby, and I pray for our family all the time. Our lives have changed. Praying brought my family even closer together.

I study the word more. Making my request known, I was taught by praying to God. My prayer life has grown. I find myself praying every day all day. If I pray, I know my prayers have answered. I surround myself with Christ like-minded people who have supported me through rough times and prayed for my family. The Launch Family is ready to do God's work. In the past, I had friends who were real friends, and some were not. My church family is fantastic. I no longer have to second guess who my friends are. The family at the Launch church is now my family. If I need prayer, the entire Church will pray for me. The Launch Church pray together as one. Since my first day at the Launch, just to name a few, I have been delivered from depression and rejection. I feel so much better, no worries. I have seen other members set free, and they felt great!

During the first month of my membership, there was a ninety-day challenge to read the entire bible. I did it! There was a bible discussion to help us understand the word of God if I have questions I know where to look in the bible. If I have some concerns, I know where to look in the bible manual. I'm not a bible scholar, but I'm on my way. I am learning what God's plan is for my life. I have learned the character that God wants me to have.

I am who God says I am—not being ashamed of my gifts I can walk in the authority of God. There was a time that I was ashamed of praying in front of a crowd. I thought people were grading me on the words that I used for prayer. I felt like I did not pray long enough or loud enough. There was a time I was afraid to preach in front of a crowd. In the past, there was a time I was scared to speak to people about God. I'm not afraid to now.

In the past, I have had some good teachers and some bad ones. The bad ones affected me more. It was hard being in ministry then later being mistreated and ignored. Today, I can honestly say God has placed me under great leadership. When I have questions and concerns, the Pastors will make themselves available to me to answer my questions. My Pastors see where I am spiritually and encourage me to grow. They give me the tools to help me find my way. Suggesting Christian study guides and weekly bible study, properly giving me correction when needed. I have seen my Pastors go to war on my behalf through prayer.

There was a time I wanted to give up on Church altogether, never wanting to step foot in a church again. Some of the churches I attended were so far from helping people. They were about making themselves look good. Practicing criticism, and at times band you from their group. In helping each other, they were not. When the word of God was preached, I attended Church, but the people were not listening. I stayed home hurt by how Christian people would treat me. I began to hear the word of God online; this helps a lot. It did not feel the same as a fellowship. I also learned more about myself. Some of this hurt I put on myself by accepting anything and not standing up for myself and being disobedient to God. While spending my Sundays at home, I decided not to visit or joined a church unless God led me to it. I did not want to waste my time in a place where I could not grow. I prayed and waited.

Sometimes your emotions get you in trouble. As I sit in minister class, I have seen how the instructor would train the other student differently than he would teach me. There were rules the student had to follow, but they also received special privileges, and I did not. I was tired of being left out of activities, discussions. I had to ask questions to understand the assignment. Separate instructions were given to the rest of the class. I felt like I was failing. I watch others moving into positions that they were not ready for, and I was left out. I felt so angry and frustrated. I got to the point where every little thing would frustrate me. I allowed frustration to make me feel worthless. This emotion turned inward in my body, and I began to get physically sick. The headaches, high blood, pressure aches, and pain in the body and anxiety.

I have learned not to allow situations to frustrate me. I have learned how to speak up and stand up for myself. Deliverance from the frustration will enable me to be free. I am stress-free of anxiety. I realized that I could not stress myself out by doing several things at one time. I can't allow people to stress me out and make me feel guilty. I have to take my time and do things right.

Singing in the choir, I realized that It had to be more to this. I wasn't using the gifts that God has given to me was not being used. I was always frustrated. I even doubted who God called me to be. I began to believe people when they called me names and put me down. I also stop communicating with people. I would just talk to my family. I would see other ministers prosper in their calling and feel bad that I was not. I was told to visit other churches and socialized to make myself known, so I would get invited to preach. God did not ask me to do this. Eventually, I felt better. While waiting, I studied the Word of God, spent more time with my family, and worked on my spiritual walk with God and became more health conscious. I believed God would send me to the right

Church. God encouraged me by placing in my life on this journey. God also sent people to call me to have a bible study over the phone. My family supported me by giving me words of encouragement. While at work, my husband would send me encouraging scriptures; this made me feel better. At this time, I was trying to let go of all the Church hurt from childhood to adulthood.

I could not do this alone. I realized that I needed help and trying not to fall into depression again. I began to trust people to help me. I joined the Launch Church, and I got what I needed.

As a member of The Launch Church, I began to feel needed and worthy. I knew God sent me to the right Church. I have learned how to be happy with myself. No longer depressed or worrying all the time. I fell at peace and ready to work in the Gods Kingdom. I have confidence in myself because God loves me. I am a child of God. I'm living in Victory! No longer afraid to love others and me. God has given me a sound mind and a peaceful heart. God has changed my life. God has healed my broken heart.

God has shown me that I can do great things.

I was led to these scriptures to read daily for encouragement,

The Lord is My Light and Salvation, whom shall I fear, whom shall I be afraid. Psalms 27:1. The Lord is my Shepard I shall Not Want. Psalms 23:1. I can do all things through Christ

Jesus who strengthens me Philippians 4:13. God did not give us the spirit of fear but a spirit of power and love and a sound mind. 2 Timothy 1:7.

The Moment I let God in my life all the way, I gave him my complete Yes! The way God moved in my life made a high impact on me. I am a better person, much more reliable, and wiser. My total being is because of God. Everything I do glorify through Him. I don't talk the same way.

I don't eat the same foods. I don't praise and worship the same way. What I do in everyday life is done to please God. Glory be to God! I am free at last! Walking into my calling. **YES, LORD YES!**

JASMINE RICHARDSON

IT'S TIME TO WAKE UP PROPHET –
SHE WILL DO GREAT THINGS

Was born and raised on the east side of San Antonio Texas. She is the daughter of Ellen Richardson and Michael Greene. She is the first from her parents, followed by her little sister Breanna Greene. Jasmine was a perfect attendance and most improved student throughout elementary, middle school and high school. Her high school was Sam Houston where she became the senior vice President, varsity cheerleader, captain of the pep squad, varsity choir and Gamma sigma (girl Scout) participate. In June 2011 she graduated with her high school diploma with honors of three years of French.

A couple of months after high school Jasmine gave birth to her first son Melvin, a year after that she birthed her second son Jaden. Ms. Richardson was a server at Chili's and a sales associate for a couple of clothing stores. While working at Melrose clothing store part time she was a part time student at a trade school. Where she earned her (CDA)

Child Development Associates. From there on she became an Early Head Start teacher at Ella Austin Community Center. Sometime after that she gave birth to her third son Jeremy in February 2017. He was born with ABS syndrome, he was affected on his left side, with a shorthand and a missing part of his feet. A couple of months after he was born Jasmine reconnected with Ella Austin and became a Preschool Teacher. Nine months after reconnecting with Ella Austin, Jasmine left and became a work study at St. Philip's College and pursued her education

Six years after high school in 2017, Jasmine began her journey at St. Philip's College. There she earned two certificates of recognition at St. Philip's College literary magazine, known as Tiger Paws. That was her first time her poems were published, and she became an author In Fall 2019. She became president of an organization at St Philip's College called, I AM WOMAN. Ms. Richardson is still the president until the end of spring semester 2020. She will graduate spring 2020 with her associates of teaching. Then transferring to A&M San Antonio to complete her teaching degree. Jasmine is also the president of the parent committee at her eight and seven year olds school. She has been a very involved and active parent since day one. She has many experiences of being the president of the parent community throughout her older two boys earliest school life.

Ms. Richardson was a member at Calvary Baptist Church where she praised dance for 12 years until November 2019. She and her three boys are a current member at The Launch Church San Antonio. Jasmine is currently the second chair of the youth department and the second chair of the dance department.

Throughout her parenting life she has been a single mother for five years. Throughout her struggle she continues to pursue her education and her children's education as well. There's no stopping God from working in her and her children 's life.

My Testimony

When I was young, my mother, my sister, and I lived in my grandmother's home, which was the family home. I can't tell you when I started to feel different than other family members. All I can say, is that it happened when I was a young girl. I remember when my grandmother's Church came over and they would form a circle around the living room. My sister and I would stand near the circle and look at each other while praise and worship was going on. At that time all I knew was just them praying. The voices were getting louder and louder and deeper and the whole house seemed to just fill with their prayers throughout the house in a voice thanking God and praising God for who he is and what you have done for them. I remember I was just laughing and giggling all through the circle because I really didn't know what was going on. I just knew a bunch of people getting in a circle holding hands and stuff. As I grew older, I understood they were praising God and worshipping God plus speaking in tongues. Funny right!?

The house that my grandmother owned with her sister, was lived in by my great grandparents, my grandmother's sister's daughter and a bunch of other people that I never met. My grandmother and her sister helped a lot of women and their children when they didn't have places to go.

In the dining room, which was called the computer room, I used to be on the computer at night time and so mostly all the lights were turned off. I would always get this cold sensation around me and I would get the creeps because the rest of the house was not cold, and I didn't have an air conditioner or fan blowing on me. I also remember seeing clothes that were hanging up in the room on the wall swinging back and forth with no air blowing in the room. I would get completely spooked and would run into my grandmother's room jump in the bed and close my eyes. Of course, I never knew what it was I was experiencing at that age. I thought that I was a weird kid in an old spooky house. Grownups in my family never explained to me what was going on and I just felt like they were brushing me off.

As I grew older, I started experiencing different things at night when my bedroom door was closed. I would see shadows underneath the door as if they were in the hallway. I started to investigate if I was tripping or if somebody was actually walking in the hallway back and forth. As I said before, while I was growing up, I thought I was a weird kid or one that had one heck of imagination. It was a weird feeling! I couldn't tell my mom because I always felt like I was brushed off. I felt crazy! My grandmother would always tell stories about the things that she would experience. For instance, her and her sister would be in the room talking and all of a sudden, they would see children running into the bathroom, but to be clear those kids were spirits. Of course, I was amazed at what I was hearing. But I didn't quite understand what was going on or what she saw. She would always tell me that she was filled with the Holy Ghost and that is why she experienced so many things. I kind of always knew that my grandma didn't tell me the whole story or didn't explain everything down to a T. Don't ask how, I just knew. I just didn't understand why!?

So, going through school I kind felt different from other children. I had low self-esteem and I would get picked on, and bullied until I started sticking up for myself. I was always so nice, and people would take advantage of my kindness and who I was. For some odd reason I would always look at people and watch them just to figure out if they were good company or bad company. Most times I was right, so I would befriend those who I felt had a good heart. I just thought it was just nature's way, never thought it was anything special going on. I always thought I needed a boyfriend, so for every grade I always had somebody. Most of the time the ones I picked were no good. As I think back on my life I see that I was looking for a male figure to be with me because my Dad wasn't present in my life. He was there in the household, but not involved as a Dad should be. So, there I was, still in middle school playing with barbie dolls and my pink tall barbie doll house, imagining like every other little girl would. Just to find a prince that would love me and to have this magical love and magical life. When one relationship would die, somehow, I'd pick up another relationship. I was always looking for love, for security, without even realizing what I was doing.

As I got into high school. I found myself being interested in one particular guy. I didn't even know who he was or know anything about him. He would seem to just always pop up after the first time I met him. So, after that we begin dating. Now when I say this next part you will probably think I was dumb, but hey! The first few weeks of dating this guy I kind of felt like something wasn't right. Just hearing his soft words just kind of pulled me in. Just for the record, if you're spirit says NO, please run (laugh out loud). For a long time, I felt like I was on top of the Moon; this was the best relationship I ever had. But, things started to crumble really fast! Y'all know the high school sweetheart story? The varsity cheerleader and the varsity football player had this on and off relationship. Blah blah blah! That was us! It felt like I needed him and that was it, period. Nobody could tell me anything! I MEAN NOTHING AT ALL! I always had a hard time with our COUNTLESS breakups. I thought it was normal, you know. I just couldn't understand why I was just so crazy over this one guy.

Time went on and I learned I was pregnant two days before my high school graduation. What a graduation gift! I say that in panic, confusion and excitement with all the chaos that was going on. If you're talking about a rough pregnancy, Oh, I can stand up and testify that my pregnancy was the rockiest and hardest that many people have ever seen. I was so sick day and night. I couldn't eat anything, I couldn't hold anything down, I couldn't even drink water and have it stay in my tummy. I was so weak and frail, I would just lay on the couch all day in depression, because I didn't know what was going on! The good thing about it was the baby was healthy the whole time, even though it seemed like the baby was sucking the life out of me. A negative part was I went through this trauma by myself without the baby's father. Just to give you a preview of the trials and tribulations with this relationship. I didn't have a support system from him when I was pregnant, which was three times. Don't worry, I'll get to the other two babies in just a second. There was cheating involved and some talking down took place. As I already mentioned, I ended up having two more babies with the same pregnancy conditions. You're probably thinking I'm crazy for allowing my body to go through such a traumatic time. Yeah, I thought the same thing.

The second baby that I had was during a time when we weren't together. He was actually in a relationship with somebody else and I thought the only way to get him back was to have intercourse with him. I know you are probably looking at me like WOW, how could you? Trust me I never did anything like this in my entire life. But when I learned that I was pregnant it was too late to go back. Sometime after our second child was born we got back together, and then we did the on and off thing a couple times. After this last breakup, I told myself I was done with the crap. I ended up going to a trade school. I didn't have a car, so everything I did was on the bus. I worked part-time at Melrose and then I would go to school a couple of days out the week. After receiving my certificate of Child Development Associates, I was offered a position at an Early Head Start program. I never made so much money in my entire life. A single mother with two kids having a good income. Baby let me tell you the money was rolling. I wasn't on any Section 8 program at the time, so me and my boys got ourselves an apartment. I just knew it was such an amazing blessing from God. It was like once I left the mess alone, blessings would flow, and they did BIG TIME!!

I'm sorry, did I ever mention that when I was working for Melrose my boss portrayed herself as a prophet and I believed her. God knows I believed her, because a lot of things that she said came true. One major thing was that my kid's dad would come back to me and marry me. So now you are probably thinking this girl is crazy, just know my heart was set on a journey. It wasn't the right way, but hey what can I say. So as you can figure it out, I let my children's dad come visit them and I noticed quickly that things were turning bad. His focus wasn't so much on the kids as much as it was on me. Soon after, sickness crept in and after three E.R. trips I was told I was pregnant. Not too much longer after that everything started to crash down. It seemed like God was just taking everything back because I did wrong and didn't keep my eyes on him. He gave me everything that I asked for and I turned around and did wrong, man what a sad time that was.

Let's rewind back before I allowed their dad to come. I was an Early Head Start teacher. I loved my job not only for the money but for what I was doing, changing lives and teaching young minds. Even though everything seemed to be going well, I noticed that for some reason some people didn't like me and I couldn't understand why. I was and still am sweet as pie but people made me feel sad and confused. People often told me throughout my life. I had a glow about me! I never really knew what that meant. I just walk to my own beat and smile all the time, that's just me. Soon my happiness at work became my frustration. A group of women at work were attacking me left and right. All I could do was go to the restroom, cry and pray to God that this madness would go away. Well, turns out instead of them leaving, I had to leave because I was sick and pregnant and couldn't even work. You see how God turns it around! Hmm!

After my nine months of being pregnant. I had Jeremy, which is my baby boy. The day I birthed him is the same day

I learned of his disability. He was affected all on the left side with no foot and short fingers. I had no idea about his condition. I was hurt, confused, shocked, upset and many more feelings in one. I was so angry at God. I mean angry to a certain extent to where I was lost. How could God allow this to happen to me and my child? I just couldn't understand. It took me a while to process everything and to just really admire God's beauty in my child.

Yes, I had a church home and a couple of members would come to me and pray with me and for me. They told me that God didn't make mistakes and I started to attend Sunday service again. I belonged to a Baptist Church for over ten years, but I always had this feeling that I was missing something. I couldn't figure it out and the people that I would always confide in within the church seemed to just worship and pray to God and talk about his goodness and that was it. To me I was like is that it? You go to church to hear the announcements, the choir sing, the praise dancers dance, a sermon and then you go home. Most times I didn't feel full. I just felt content until the next Sunday. Sounds funny right, I know!

One day, I got invited to a church and I didn't know what to expect. I heard good things about it meaning things I never heard or seen before. I have to admit I was kind of excited because I didn't know what I was walking into. The first time me and my kids went, I have to admit, I was listening to the word but I was also looking at everybody else. You know how you go somewhere new and you want to check out everybody before you start saying hi haha! The person that invited me was my best friend's mother, I call her my Godmother. She told me to go up for prayer and of course I was nervous, I didn't know what to expect. All I remember is this beautiful lady coming to speak to me and telling me to put my hands up. She was speaking in tongue and it was like she was talking to God but also talking to me at the same time. I remember her saying that God loves you and I love you too. As you can imagine I kept going back to receive more from God. I was hungry for his love. I was hungry for a message from him. I could remember the next time I went up to be prayed for, I was prophesied to by a young lady who looked my age. At first, I kind of looked like who is this girl? The young lady started to prophesize to me but at that time Pastor Will was casting a demon out of a lady. I have to admit I was kind of creeped out and I wanted to run for the door because I have never seen anything like that. Anyways, the young lady that prophesized to me was hugging me and started to cry. I thought to myself why is she crying? She told me you don't know how special you are, do you? I looked at her like WHAT! She continued and told me that God favors me, I would be a leader of this church, this Christmas will be one of the best Christmas's that we would ever have and so many other things. Let me remind you, I still belonged to another church, but just kept going back to The Launch Church. I just kept wrestling with myself, I had been with this Baptist Church for so long and they have done great things for me and my family, but this new Church makes me feel full and closer to God then I have ever been. Shortly after, I gave my YES TO GOD!

Let me tell you, my kids got more than enough gifts for Christmas and the blessings just kept coming and coming out of nowhere. On our big Launch Party that we had on New Year's Eve, it was announced that I was the second chair of the Youth Department. Not only that, sometime later I became second chair of the Praise Dance Ministry. I learned who I am, God made me a Prophet!!! Slowly but surely, I started to experience different things like hearing things, seeing things, and having dreams. I showed signs of a Prophet before I knew my destiny. Earlier I mentioned I always thought I was a weird person, but no it was meant for me to hear things and see things. Giving God my YES changed everything in my life. People that meant no good in my life started to be pinpointed out in different situations through God for a reason. Light shined upon the confusion I felt when I was pregnant and so severely sick with all three of my boys. They are destined to be so powerful when they grow up. I'm raising a Prophet, Pastor and a Palmist. THANK YOU JESUS! Remember, I was dealing with so much confusion with my kid's dad and I told you I always felt like I needed him. Guess what!? Soul ties were cut on New Year's Eve during our Launch party. I was prophesied that my husband is coming and that he would provide more love than me and the kids ever had unconditionally!!!

Giving God my YES means everything to me. Thinking that I had to control how my life should go, when really God is in control. He has so many wonderful things for each and every one of us. All we have to do is give him a complete YES, believe and have faith that our father above is who he said he is. God of God's, King of Kings and Almighty by himself. Coming to The Launch Church helped me open the doors to my destiny. My kids and I will forever be grateful that God put The Launch Church together with amazing Pastors' Lee and Taundra Williams to lead the way. God, I give you my YES a thousand times. The prophet in me is finally waking up and I will do wonderful things!! THANK YOU JESUS!

EBONI MOORE
I"VE GOT A TESTIMONY

Although Eboni was not raised in a church she always had a heart for God and his people at the age of 28 Eboni was filled with the Holy Ghost and the evidence of speaking in tongues under the Pastor Alonzo and Diane Hurt she found purpose in following Christ. Eboni always knew there was something special about her and how different she was from the rest of the kids she was around. When she was just 5 years old she used to play church with her first cousin Jameel Moore, Later when she turned 11, she would go with her friend to her mother bishop house, while all the other kids was playing on the instruments and in the chairs Eboni was standing behind the pulpit telling her friends how good God was and how the world need to change. She never imagined the gifts and anointing she had inside of her until God started using her in ways she could not have done herself. Once Eboni started seeing the favor and calling of God on her life she started practicing her true walk with Christ to be as close to Jesus.

She always had a heart for Gods people and saw the good in everybody before she started her walk with God she would have friends over and talked about the bible and how to make a plan to better the world. Eboni is eager to please God in any way that she can her hopes and dreams is to be more and more like Christ each and every day. She also learned that over the years her trial and errors made her to be the strong woman that she is today. She is looking forward to what God has in store not only for her but also for you, she believes that every lesson is a blessing once you make it out and learn from it. Eboni lives by the quote' I can do all things through Christ who strengthens me" Philippians 4:13 KJV". Although she comes off shy put God in the middle and she comes alive, she is driven by his spirit and helping his people that are in bondage.

Eboni is currently studying for her Bachelor's in Theology in Christian Ministries currently she does not have a minor and is seeking guidance from God on which way he wants her to go. Eboni have a passion for helping women, and children mostly the ones that have been abused from some sort. She plans on continuing to fight this battle of Faith for her and her son Carl and daughter Mir'Kale to become one with God and for God. Eboni can do anything she put her mind to. Once she gets started, she goes until she finishes. She is dedicated to complete the purpose she has here on earth, just to hear God say" Well done my good and Faithful Servant."

My Testimony

There is never a perfect way to start when it comes to telling the goodness of God. When it comes to my life and even yours if you know it or not. I am not able to tell my whole life story so I will just give you the pieces that lead to my "COMPLETE YES" throughout my life I went to church off and on, with my grandma and my aunt Shirley who have both gone to be with the Lord. Even though when I got older, I wasn't consistent with my walk with God I had them seeds planted. The bible states in Proverbs 22:6 "Train up a child in the way he should go and when he is old, he will not depart from it."

I was called inside the womb. I fought with my identity for a very long time as a matter of fact I am still learning how to identify myself through Gods eyes. All my life I have been living my life to what the world has made me out to be. Deep down inside I knew I was different, I thought different from everyone, I looked at things different from everyone, I mean there was a ME that I was trying to figure out and was looking for answers in all the wrong places.

I was sucked into the world at a young age because I didn't know better, I thought I was supposed to be a certain way, talk a certain way or think a certain way because I was black. There I was pregnant at 17 I knew nothing about nothing, a baby having a baby. One thing I did believe in was prayer, the only thing about that is I only prayed when I got in trouble. Although that is not the best thing to do at least I can say I started somewhere, I can say that now because now I live a life of prayer.

So here I am in a world I don't know too much about and bringing a life into, my son's father was the first guy I had ever been with thinking I was in love because he gave me the attention I never had growing up. I did not like him at all in the beginning because he was a bully. One day his cousin begged me to hook up with him, something inside of me did not want to do it, but me being a people pleaser I went with it.

I found out I was pregnant when he went to jail, so I became a single mother as he missed the whole pregnancy. He was released when my son was six months old. He got out and listened to rumors that I was cheating on him while he was locked up, so the abuse started. He was physically/verbally abusive. I had a hard time leaving because I thought that was part of being in a relationship because that's all I'd seen growing up, this went on for about four years. In that time, I got introduced to marijuana, and clubbing, I was finally being accepted by what I thought was friends.

I finally got away from him when my son turned 4 years old. He got locked up again and I moved to Texas by force. The Feds kicked in my door looking for someone I was dating at the time who lived in the building next to me, (Yes I've sold drugs at one point in time) by the grace of God I was in a different state at the time, so I had no choice but to move to Texas to be with my mom and siblings, Still in the dark I came down here and had to fight the system (CPS) for my son for seven years. I blamed everybody but myself.

See there is power of life and death in the tongue, for years I used tell my son he was going to baby YDC (Youth Detention Center) and I would tell his father I was going to send him to be with CPS (Child Protective Services). At the time I was smoking weed and clubbing. My house was the party house, I had a foul mouth, you name it. I look back now and thank God for his Grace and Mercy. I was addicted to marijuana I mean if I didn't have it I was an evil witch (with a B) it was controlling me, I got to the point when I rolled up a blunt, I would pray that God deliver me from it because to be honest I wasn't even getting high anymore Just dirtying up my system and spending money I didn't have, paying somebody else bills. So, I told myself until I get delivered from smoking, whatever I spend on a bag of marijuana I was going to give the same amount to the Church.

Whatever Church came on TV, I sowed into that ministry, what they did with the money was between them and God I said if I can give the weed man money, I can give money to the house of God and I did just that. As this journey was not a smooth ride, I thank God he kept me through it all. I have made a lot of mistakes on this walk; I didn't know what to do or how to do it I learned by trial and error. I was a single mom, miles away from my family. I found myself trying to fit in and be accepted by other families to fill the emptiness of my own family just to be rejected and talked about.

I remember going through a season of depression where I didn't know what to do. The people I went to or tried to talk to either just talked about me or pushed me away. I was on my own, all my life people have been looking at me and treating me like my name doesn't hold any weight. And because I didn't know who I was; I allowed them to treat me as such then I started acting like the person they made me out to be, little did they know there are gifts inside of me that may answer some of the questions they worry God with.

I remember on my 25th birthday (12/31/2007) I was at the club with everybody I knew here in San Antonio, and when that ball dropped I saw everything different the people I was with they looked like strangers to me, I didn't understand it until later that God was calling me while I was in the club while I was drunk and high. So, I started reading "The Purpose Driven Life" by Rick Warren. I couldn't understand the Bible so I had to do something to see what God would want me to do. I didn't want to ask nobody what Church I should go to because everybody is going to say I should go to this type of Church because it says right here in the Bible. So,

I prayed and asked God to send me somewhere I always prayed in the name of Jesus.

The next year that's when life's trials really started happening to me. September 5, 2008, I lost my car, September 12, 2008 I lost my job, September 25, 2007 they took my son, and September 30, 2008, I lost my Section 8 voucher. After all this I was lost, It took about a month before God sent me to a Church where later I was filled with The Holy Spirit 3/26/2009, It wasn't even on a Sunday or Wednesday I was doing Elect lady hair, and she asked me "have you ever been filled with the Holy Ghost?" I didn't think I did so I said "No" she prayed for me I praised God, Next thing I knew I was in a totally different mindset, my walk changed, my talk changed, I was so covered by God that the battle I was in didn't even bother me.

At this time God was preparing me for ministry even as a baby in Christ, then life happened, I back slid did a nice moon walk with the shiny socks. I'm going to skip over some years and tell you about me saying out of my mouth that I don't want to get married anymore I just want a little girl and the father and I can co-parent. Boy did I eat those words. I got my little girl, but I went through hell and high water trying to co-parent with her father, now I told you earlier that my son father was physical and verbally abusive. My daughter's father was verbally, mentally, and emotionally, abusive along with being a bully, womanizer, and manipulator, I stayed in a family abuse center for six months off the grid to get away from him. He then sent CPS to every place my family lived in whatever state they lived in acting like he was concerned about my daughter, If I didn't do what he said he would call CPS on me which lead me to get up and leave everything behind. I now know that it was the devil that came to steal, kill, and destroy my life to keep me from focusing on my purpose.

That's exactly what happened, I was delivered from marijuana, but now I'm smoking black n mild cigars and drinking myself to numb the pain and the hurt that I bared inside, no matter how much I told him to leave me alone and be co-parents it wasn't enough anytime I tried to get on my feet he would somehow get a hold of me or pretend he want to see my daughter just to see what I was doing I better not be doing good oh let the sabotaging begin I tried to be the bigger person but he just didn't want me to do good or better than him so he tried to keep me scared or in bondage, I had to do something because I like my freedom and independency and he didn't like that. I will encourage you if you are being treated in any way that is not like the kings/queens you are please, please get out of it as soon as possible God always send signs to warn you. If you see the signs get out and get help before it's too late. Nobody should treat you like you're less than them or belittle you to make themselves feel or look better. In my case I was stripped from my confidence, self-esteem, my dreams, my hopes, my faith, my happiness, my character, you name it I was totally lost and allowed man to help me get there.

I went back to the Church where God had first sent me and got myself back together, one service we had a guest speaker, Pastor Lee Williams, he came with all this power and woke my spirit up like New Fire, He didn't even lay hands on me and I went limp, he then went on to say God wants a "YES" little did I know my life wasn't going to be the same after that day. I guess I was ready to receive the gifts in which God had anointed me to have, I started operating in hearing Gods voice myself confused me at first, until I got confirmation it was true. God started showing me things in my sleep it was scary at first I wasn't sure I wanted to have that part of the gifts, but we don't know what all our "YES" entails we have to stay ready at all times.

This journey is a process don't think for one minute because you are saved or doing the work of the Lord that you won't be tested, it's the "FAITH" that comes along with your walk that helps you get through. But I had to figure out what I was battling with and why it's keeping me from giving my "COMPLETE YES" It took me 36 years to understand my life, I finally told God enough is enough send me Lord I'll go, what is it that you want me to do. But God could not use me unless I understood my life, he had to show me who I wasn't and who I am. Once I saw the difference, I was like "ok no I don't want to be her," I grew into her from the world I can't walk in my full potential and not living like the world profiled me to be. My one desire is to be like Jesus, I want to be able to look at someone and speak over them and make things ok or to help boost up their faith.

God sent me to another Church where the Pastor broke my life down from childhood and he didn't even know anything about me. But in that God showed me "ME" he helped me understand my faults, my lack of wisdom and knowledge, and even where the generational curses that was over my life. I was still a child in some areas because I had trauma in that part of my life, so I was stuck there. God had to train me to be mature and live and not just survive or exist. I'm still learning right now. When I tell you, God took everything out of me and allowed me to start over. Complete renovation.

Learning how to deal with rejection and not allowing it to hinder my life. I had to learn not to live by acceptance it's ok not to be accepted I mean even Jesus was rejected, mocked, laughed at, lied on etc., what makes me different, I had to say Lord I no longer care what people say about me or what they think, I'm going to live for you and only you, God showed me that I was trying to fit in with everybody or wanted other people's approval. The only approval that matters is from God. I thank him for showing me that, don't get me wrong it is a lonely world right now, but I have my peace and my kids with me, and now my new Church family I'm going to make it through.

Let me also add it is very important to have a support system, we need each other and we should all love one another, don't be like I was giving everybody the benefit of the doubt and just accepting anything and everybody all they had to do was accept me, little did I know that came with snakes rats, and spirits. I pray for genuine friends that are trying to get it right every day because none of us are perfect but if people want to live a warm life style I don't want to be a part of that unless it's warm because they are starting the new life but pure genuine love friendship, sisterhood, brotherhood is the way God want it.

This is just a short part of my story I pray it Bless you well, and you too can lean on giving God YOUR "COMPLETE YES', you are not alone on this journey keep looking to the hill from where your help comes from and see where God will leads you. Stir up the gift inside of you.

CHIFFON D. TURNER

A CRY FOR MY YES

Chiffon D. Turner is a single mother to a beautiful one year old little girl. Chiffon says she has learned and is patiently waiting to be a wife to an anointed Pastor prophet. She is a first time Author, A Pastor in training, Prophet of fire for such a time as this, an intercessor, a praise dancer, the daughter of Pastor's Lee Williams III and Taundra Williams and most of all a daughter of the Most High God! She is the oldest of five, has a passion for helping those who cannot help themselves. She is a multi-entrepreneur on the rise, she has recently pursued the opening of her First Adult Daycare. She has extensive experience working with adults with intellectual disabilities, and additionally has been serving in church her whole life. Her prayer to God is that her YES to God will encourage others to come to Christ as she did.

My Testimony

Have you ever wondered, wow!? I actually have a choice to tell God yes or no? The creator of the universe? Telling God Yes is not just saying yes and expecting him to do the rest for you. This Yes journey is a lifestyle. The Holy Bible states There hath no temptation taken you but such as is common to man: but God is faithful, who will not suffer you to be tempted above that ye are able; but will with the temptation also make a way to escape, that ye may be able to bear it. (KJV 1 Cor. 10:13) In other words God will never let you fail. He's so faithful that he will never let you experience anything that he knows you cannot handle. When telling God Yes, it's not just saying "Yes God!" It's saying Yes God with my mind, body and soul. Yes, to his will, yes to everything he has for me. Telling God Yes does come with some tough battles, I had to change a lot about myself to follow Christ the way I needed to. I had to change the crowd of people that I accompanied, during my transformation I felt like it was hard to do. That's why it took me so long to tell God Yes, I felt like I wasn't going to be able to "Live" my life.

Before telling God Yes, I was living my life carelessly. From being a child who grew up in church you would think I'd never mess up right? I grew up in a church where pretty much the majority of my family attend, from being a church girl knowing right and wrong I still chose to do "ME. Drinking and smoking and going to clubs and still going to church acting like what I was doing wasn't wrong! I was the type to do whatever, if it made me feel good I would do it. Not understanding that the more wrong I did the quicker it was leading me straight to hell! Thinking ok well God says he forgives all sins, so I can do whatever I want I got time. Not realizing that my days were being numbered! It's not just saying yes, my actions had to change having sex outside of marriage because it "feels good"! Drinking any and everything I could if it got me tipsy I drank it. If it made me feel numb, I took it. Not only was I doing drugs, but I used being a college student who was financially struggling as an excuse to sell drugs. I started hanging around people who did drugs as well, knowing that this was a crowd I was not supposed to be around. So, because getting high wasn't enough for me I started taking pills on top of that, not realizing I could've ended my life at any giving moment! God was most definitely not pleased with me, seeing me do all the things I was doing. And he still allowed me to see another day, I started having sex with men trying to have relationships with them. I was just out being wild and not caring about what the outcome was or could have been. Because (YOU ONLY LIVE ONCE YOLO) right! Hanging with girls who meant me no good. It caused my relationship with family members who meant everything to me to grow apart. Sometimes we must look back on why we ended up in the place or situation we're in today. A lot of times it's not because of what someone did or said to us. It is our own selves; I have a mind of my own I chose to do the things I did. I chose to hang with the wrong people and started doing the same things everyone else did. Why? Because I wanted to fit in, I wanted everyone to like me, I didn't want to be left out. I felt like I had to be with the in crowd. As a child my mother used to tell me, You're picked out to be picked on. At that time, I didn't understand what that meant. Really, I didn't understand until my adult years. What it means is God chose me! Of course, we all are chosen but, the calling and purpose for my life is totally different than everyone else. How do you find out what your calling and purpose is that God has for your life? It comes with telling God yes and meaning everything with a sincere heart. There were so many issues I had going on in my body. I was always sick, and while doing these things to my body I was not aware of the trauma I could have experienced. God is so merciful that in spite of the wrong we do he still loves us he still cares. But just because God is a loving God, does not mean that I got away with the things I was doing. The Holy Bible states: Be not deceived; God is not mocked: for whatsoever a man soweth, that shall he also reap. (KJV Gal. 6:7) In other words I did not get away with the things I did. I suffered for five years; my mom always says, "Sin will make you pay more than you have to pay and make you stay longer than you have to stay." I couldn't keep a job and everywhere I applied no one would hire me. I applied at pizza joints and burger joints. Places that I knew I was overqualified for, because I couldn't find a job. I couldn't pay my bills. I couldn't pay my car note. I started applying for loans just to have money to live. I was so extremely embarrassed to tell my parents on how bad I was struggling. I was in a very overwhelming situation. During that time I met my ex-husband. We got married and during our marriage, everything that could go wrong did. Neither of us could keep a job. It didn't matter how good we were on the job. It seemed like it was just so hard to make ends meet. My marriage lasted barely a year, everything seemed too good to be true. His words were as smooth as Tennessee whisky. I fell quickly for him. I was going through so much. And it was all because of my disobedience and I didn't even realize it. Disobedience will only get you so far, Because of the free will God gives us. It's our own self choices to do whatever we want but does not change the fact that he called me, and I heard the call. That's where disobedience comes in. After getting a divorce I lost my home and my car and I had to move back home with my parents, I was very ashamed to go back home. I felt like I would never get on my feet and be independent. I had goals that I wanted to fulfill, and nothing went according to plan. During that time, I had finally got a job and started working again. It seemed like the sun was starting to shine again in my life, not until I started spending my money irresponsibly and lost my car again. Right after that I got hurt on the job and contracted a MRSA infection, having this infection almost cost me my life. I got so sick so quickly the infection was spreading so fast I had to have emergency surgery. I felt defeated and I wanted to give up on everything. Not understanding why I'm going through so much is because of my disobedience, it wasn't until I became pregnant with my daughter, when I knew I was going through so much was because of my disobedience. God began to warn me through my mother, my mother would talk to me and warn me countless times about how I need to give God my yes and stop running. I ignored her because I was going through so much, I felt like I still haven't got the chance to live my life the way I wanted to. So, in order for me to sit down and shut up, something had to happen. At four months pregnant with my daughter, I got into a really bad car accident and almost lost my and my child's life. I was forced to sit down. When she came into this world, I couldn't have imagined doing the things I was doing with a little girl looking up to me. I couldn't live another day knowing that I'm responsible for my daughter's soul as well. I had to make a difference and surrender everything to God. When I gave God my Yes I meant every tear. Every cry, every scream telling God yes! And to know that God hears me when I call him is more than enough. He values my worth; he uses me in every way. God doesn't just use me he strengthens me, he cares for me, he loves me, he provides for me. My God is all that and more! I developed a personal relationship with God, it takes seeking his face crying out to him sleepless nights. If having eternal life with God is important to you, you have to take time out. And tell God yes! I had to change my actions and my frame of mind. Changing the way you think is important as well, an idle mind is the devil's workshop. When I made up my mind that I will serve the Lord no matter what. I no longer felt like I wanted to be a part of everyone else, I started my own path. Because I chose to follow God, doesn't mean that I don't get tempted with things. It's up to you to allow yourself to be tempted. Temptation does come my way and with the temptation there's always a door of escape. And God gave me the authority over the enemy. My mind is made up that no matter what it is, how good it looks or feels. I will continue to say yes to God until Christ returns. When on this level with Christ we may have obstacles that come our way, but one thing is for sure as God says it in his word that he takes care of us. The Holy Bibles states: And even to your old age I am he; and even to hoar hairs will I carry you: I have made, and I will bear; even I will carry, and will deliver you. (KJV Isa. 46:4) Meaning from being in my mother's womb until the day I die, God is with me and takes care of me. When my daughter was born it was so important to me that my daughter knew Jesus Christ. Transforming my life is a must. I was done being lost, my soul being saved is important to me, it took me a long time to come to Christ. Because I knew I was called to the ministry, but I just didn't know what part of the ministry. I was afraid to be in front of everyone, but because this is not just my soul this is my daughter's soul as well. If I wasn't going to do this for myself, I had to do it for my daughter. When I became a part of The Launch church, I went through deliverance. This is when I took a 180 and turned my life completely around! I made up my mind no more will I live to please others. No more will I live for acceptance of man. Upon telling God Yes, I made a vow to celibacy. It was very hard at the beginning and I didn't think I would be able to keep my promise, there were times that I almost slipped. But just the thought of breaking a promise to God made me terrified for my soul. I had men approach me who was a sight for sore eyes. I made up in my mind that I will wait until God sends me my husband. A God ordained marriage is what I want, it doesn't matter how long it'll take. I told God Yes I will wait. Once I became a part of The Launch Church, I found out my true calling, learning that my purpose is to be a pastor in the ministry. I was feeling so overwhelmed with joyful emotions to know that God chose me to lead his people. To know that God chose me is an honor, despite my background God still chose me! To be in God's will is the most amazing feeling. When I told God yes to whatever he has for me, to whoever he's called me to be in the kingdom. He favors me, he loves me, and he cares for me. He keeps his promises to me! Telling God yes was the best decision I have ever made. I've just started out on this journey, and to see the blessings that God has bestowed on my life in this short period of time is amazing. I say this to you who are struggling to decide to tell God Yes, if you give God your hand and let him lead you. I promise you it will be well worth it! Never give up and remember to keep the faith.

MADLYN CHASE

THE FIGHT IN MY MIND!

Madlyn was born and raised in San Antonio, Texas. She graduated East Central High School in 2010, and months later joined the United States Army as a Food Service Specialist in April 2011. After a few years she was honorably discharged from her military service and returned back home to Texas. In December 2015, she decided to attend Cosmetology School and obtain her cosmetology license. There she found her passion for hair styling and beauty. She fell in love with making her clients feel beautiful about themselves. Her clients looked to her as a confidant for advice. The Lord would speak to her, and show her what was going on in their lives. Madlyn was driven by passion for the women and clients that would come. They were battered and bruised just like her, and that's why her business was created. Sheer Imperfections Hair & Beauty was created. Her slogan says, "There's nothing too flawed for God". She believes that it doesn't matter how broken you are, and God can fix anything. She says, "God changed her life in a matter of months, and he can change everyone else's life too." Madlyn also has six children and is a single parent. She has three boys and three girls is who she cares for. She loves her children and they love her. They are the reason for her season and things would not be the same if she would have never had them. Madlyn and her family came to The Launch Church in 2019. She gave God her "Yes" and never looked back. God is truly the redeemer in her life and deliverer. Her hopes and dreams are to fulfill the will of God for her life, and that her family will follow. After all you train up a child in the way they should go, and if one turns their heart to God the whole house shall be saved.

My Testimony

Mental health illnesses have a real impact on people all around the world including me. From my teenage years, I struggled with mental health issues that affected me going into my adult years. I had good days, bad days, and blank days. My good days were my favorite days because things would go well. My bad days were the worst days, and the ones that I was the most emotional or angry. My blank days were just like they sounded blank, and on these days, I was very lazy and did not want to do anything at all. Depression is one of those things at times you cannot explain to anyone. It may seem like talking about your issues can help, but sometimes you don't want to talk. You just want to be free. You see the real battle is what we face in our minds. One thing I can tell you for sure is that if you are not in a good mental space then you can throw your spiritual and physical health out the window. Everyone needs their mind to be able to function, but what do you do when your mind can not function? The only thing you can do is pray. When things do not make sense pray! When things go bad pray! When you don't know what to do, pray! Everything is not always going to make sense. Prayer is our way of communicating with God and getting answers to who, what, when, where and why. God is the ultimate healer and deliverer from ourselves, and that includes our minds. When we are anxious and feel oppressed by depression we can fight through prayer and intercessory to get to God and petition to him what we need. You might ask how do I know these things? Because I suffered for a very long time until one day, I decided that I wanted something different. I wanted a change. I did not know how it was going to happen, but I knew I wanted God to help me do it. So, I gave him a Yes! Well, what does that mean when you give God a "Yes"? Well let me tell you how this happened. When I came to The Launch Church SA I came with an open heart and mind. At this point in my life I was just fed up with everything that had been happening and I needed a change. I was in a toxic relationship at the time that was draining me mentally, emotionally and spiritually. I mean can you imagine everyday feeling like life was being squeezed out of you. That is what it was like for me. I was severely depressed, suicidal in my thoughts, and I mean I literally wanted to die. It was horrible. I thought that I would never leave this man, and I would never get married again because I had so many children. I was desperate for help. My spiritual life seemed like it was dimming every day. I say this because Jesus is the light in our lives right, and if his spirit wants to dwell and live in us that can't happen when we've got things that are not of God inside of us. According to The Bible, the scripture says, "Do you not know that your bodies are temples of the Holy Spirit, who is in you, whom you have received from God? You are not your own; you were bought at a price. Therefore, honor God with your bodies." - 1 Corinthians 6:19-20.

In order for us to walk in the fullness of God we must not defile our temples. What does that mean? It means we must allow God to have full access to us. God wants access to every part of our life. It is part of having a relationship with him, but sometimes we choose to idolize and put other things before God. Even though we do not mean to do these things we do them because we are human. No, you are not a bad person and no it is not too late for God to change your life. Since we are born into a world of sin we will sin, but repentance is what saves us. It also allows us to check our heart posture toward God. Even though God does know our hearts and he says in this word that our hearts are evil it does not necessarily mean he takes sin lightly. That is not true. God hates when we sin. Now, let's talk about one of the major ways you can defile your temple. One of the ways to defile your temple is through sex. Here is an example from what I experienced. When I decided to leave my ex-husband I was still married to him. Even though we were separated it did not make it okay for me to start committing adultery, which is also another way you can defile your temple. I remember the first time I had sex outside my marriage, and I felt like I wanted to die. I knew regardless of the circumstances at the time it was not an excuse to do so, but I did. Mentally, it took a toll on me because I knew it was a bad decision in the first place, but instead I convinced myself that it was not a big deal. Let me help you understand this so that you will never forget it," Your disobedience against God will kill you and everyone connected to you if you allow it to". Save yourself the sacrifice and just be obedient to God. Sex may seem like it is not a big deal, but it really is guys. It is not forbidden before marriage for nothing. Pre-Marital sex before marriage creates unwanted soul ties, agreements and covenants that you do not need. I say unwanted because sometimes we do not want to have a connection or anything to do with a person after we have sex with them. A lot of times we realize after we have sinned it was a mistake and decide to just leave the person alone afterwards. Pre-marital sex is forbidden because it not only creates these problems for us, but it opens the door for idolatry. I bet you are wondering now how is that possible? Don't I have to worship this person like God? I am not doing anything wrong. I am sorry to say this, but that is not true. It is idolatry because you are using your body as a sacrifice to lustful desires. That's basically what you did. You are sacrificing your mind, body, spirit and soul for a simple pleasure that was created for marriage purposes only. Don't you think if God wanted us to have that he would make it known that we can have it. I will even give an example from my experience. When I met one of my children's fathers, we dated for a very short period. We moved right in together and started sleeping together.

Every day he went to school/work I would make sure that he had food, clean clothes, and even let him drive my car. Don't forget he is not my husband, but I am doing all these things for him. I am not his wife, but this is what I am doing. I am also making sure the home is comfortable and to his liking etc. First, God never said this was my husband so why am I doing all this stuff? I was idolizing this man! I was sacrificing my whole self just for him to be pleased with me. We are supposed to be pleasing God not man! Man is not God! When God is not pleased that is when you should be worried. I spent all my time idolizing a person that I did not realize I was forgetting about God. I forgot that God is a jealous God, and that he continuously punished the Israelites for Idol worship. God warned them all throughout their lives to not worship idols. The Bible says, "Put to death, therefore, whatever belongs to your earthly nature: sexual immorality, impurity, lust, evil desires and greed, which is idolatry.- Colossians 3:5. God even warns us now to not put anything before him, and that he comes first. I made myself uncomfortable and accepted things that God never told me to accept in the first place. That is a covenant agreement! Covenants are agreements that you make with someone and it is as simple as saying yes. If it is one thing God asks is for us to give him our whole entire being to him. The reason I was doing the things that I was is because I wanted to feel loved. Sex made me feel loved and wanted. I felt assured, but

I was also looking for an escape out of my mind. I did not want to be locked up in my mind anymore. I did not want to think about the negative things. I just wanted to be free of the chaos, but I just did not know how to do that. At the end of the day you have to know in your mind and believe that you are worth it. I did not know my own self-worth let alone how to love myself. God would tell me that he loves me, I am worthy, and that I deserved better all the time, but my mind at the time was just not convinced. When you do not believe who God says you are, you will start to question everything you knew about God. That my friend is an identity crisis that took root from a seed of doubt that was planted. All it takes is one seed. If you doubt God more than likely you will doubt yourself and everything you do because you have no assurance. The times we question God the most is in our time of trouble and need. When we are suffering and enduring pain, we cry out the most, but you have to believe that things will change. You have to believe that God will help, heal, and deliver you from your pharaoh. You have to talk to yourself and tell yourself who God says you are! Every day now I affirm myself who God says I am and how he sees me. I am a daughter, I am a prophet, I am a writer, I am a great mother, I am a warrior, and that is just a few of mine. When I decided to join The Launch Church, it was on the first visit I came. God asked me immediately for a commitment. I was not sure at first, but I was obedient. I said "Okay, I'll try this out." He assured me things would be different this time around. I was just happy to finally take steps toward where I needed to be. I even wrote a letter to myself that night I came home.

This is what I wrote:

Dear God,

I am so happy that I've found a place to worship you. I am also happy that I've met new people, who were looking for a new home as well. I really hope I did the right thing by joining The Launch Church. I felt I was running out of time, and I needed to commit to something. So why not make a commitment to you and clean up my life? This was me stepping out of my comfort zone. I couldn't just sit around feeling hopeless anymore. You made a way for me to come out of the darkness, and it was just a matter of me trusting. At least I took a chance on the right thing. I stepped out on faith and I trust that you will lead the way. Thank you for opening a path for me.
Love, Your Daughter.

Little did I know this was a whole process God had planned out for me. I mean literally a set up. God was waiting for me there. He waited for me to surrender my whole heart and my whole self to him. God did not force me to give my "Yes", He just waited for me to get to a place of submission and surrender, and when I finally did things turned around for me and my family. Since I had given my "Yes" to God things started changing very fast for me. It wasn't overnight, but the days came very fast. I started tithing and God kept sustaining me every time. Even when I thought I wouldn't have enough. God kept showing up to make sure I had what I needed and more. God also started giving my business ideas, and blessed me with a mentor, that would push me to be everything God said I was and more. I mean I am blessed beyond measures and so are my children. The best way I could say God dealt with me was like an onion. I had layers of things, but I had to let him peel them all of them back one at a time to get to the center of me. I needed to see the core part of me because that is where everything was hidden. The real question is how did I overcome all of this? Honestly, obedience is what saved my life. We might have our mind, will and emotions, but obedience can save us from our flesh. The way we think makes us choose, the things we are willing to do shapes our choices, and our emotions as well. If we feel like owing something we will do it, but our obedience to God is what saves us from going through whirlwinds of turmoil. Obedience is the sweetest reward God gives us.

TENA M. NALLS

AN UNCOMPROMISING YES!

Born Tena Marie Peoples in Pompano Beach, Florida, along with her five other siblings. Evangelist Tena Nalls was trained up in the nurture and admonition of holiness by her mother Rose Peoples. Although the enemy tried to thwart Gods' plan and purpose for her life and that of her twin brother, Gods' Will prevailed.

Tena's secular education took place at Tedder Elementary school and Blanche Ely High school where she graduated and obtained her HS diploma in 1993. However, more importantly was Tena's spiritual journey which began when she was baptized into Christ at the age of eight. Even at such an early age, God had anointed Tena as a songstress. Tena is very passionate about singing and has never neglected her anointing to sing.

When Tena was a teenager, she fully surrendered her life to Christ and continued her spiritual journey serving God at New Covenant Deliverance Cathedral under the leadership of

Bishop Ralph and First Lady Ida Mae Grissett of Fort Lauderdale, Florida. During her tenure there, Tena served faithfully as Choir Director, Praise and Worship Leader, and Junior Secretary. Tena and her family worshipped at New Covenant Deliverance Cathedral for nineteen years, faithfully attending Worship Service and Sunday school weekly. It was here that Tena continued to display her passion for singing. She has embraced many opportunities to minister in song to God's people. After the Peoples family had served so passionately for 19 years at New Covenant Deliverance Cathedral God released Tena into her own personal ministry of Worship.

At the tender age of 19 years God was ordering Tena's steps towards ministry in the gospel. Her obedience to the call led her to serve under Apostles T. C. and A. R. Maxwell of Faith Deliverance Tabernacle located in Fort Lauderdale, Florida. As expected, she found herself at home once again as Praise and Worship Leader, as well as choir director. As she continued to grow and mature spiritually, she was ordained and licensed as a Minister of the Gospel in 2004 by her pastor, Apostle T. C. Maxwell. As a minister of the gospel Tena taught Sunday School and participated in the Youth Ministry all with great zeal and passion for imparting the wisdoms and knowledge of God into the hearts and minds of the church youth.

Having reached the age to marry and having waited patiently upon God to fulfill His promise, God blessed Tena to meet Mr. William Grimes and after a very short courtship they were joined in holy matrimony on December 20th, 1998 and remained married until 2007 when God called His beloved son to his rest. As anyone could imagine, such life events changed Tena's course and she soon transitioned to Atlanta, Georgia. While in Atlanta Tena continued to be prepared for ministry under leadership of none other than Apostles' T.C. and A.R. Maxwell however under a newly transformed ministry, Faith Deliverance Kingdom Now Ministries.

While graciously serving at Faith Deliverance Kingdom Now Ministries in Atlanta she met her current husband Jarod Alexander Nalls Sr. and in 2012 they were joined in Holy Matrimony. In 2015 God orchestrated for the Evangelist and her husband to transition to San Antonio, Texas and immediately she took up her mantle to serve under the leadership of Bishop David and Pastor Claudette Copeland of New Creation Christian Center. Evangelist Tena continued in her passion, singing songs of Zion in the Cathedral Choir, and the Judah Praise Team.

After having served one and a half years under Pastors' Copeland tutelage, she was led to serve in an administrative capacity under Pastor Prophetess Felicia Napier Huff, and Elder Tyrann Huff in their rapidly growing ministry, The Voice Revival Center. Not only were Tena's administrative skills a great asset to the ministry, her audiovisual skills allowed the ministry to step out into social media outreach, where they are reaching numerous viewers.

After having served two and a half years under Pastor Huff's tutelage, she was led by God to serve in ministry under Pastors' Lee Williams III and Taundra Williams in their continual growing ministry, The Launch Church. Since being at The Launch, God has birthed out of her a talk session to encourage others in their Faith called What The Faith and is also now an author. She is also growing into the office of an Evangelist.

Such a talented woman of God Tena has written many songs, one of which is titled, "The Other Woman "which has showcased at the Annual Priceless Jewels Women's Conference with Apostle A.R, Maxwell in Atlanta, Georgia in 2015 until now. Evangelist Tena is also a Massage Therapist and has other interests that include. Fashion design, T-shirt design, writing books, DIY designs, and traveling to name a few.

Evangelist Tena Marie Nalls' maturity and her strong faith in God is a great credit upon her and the many leaders under which she served. She continues to purposely use her spiritual gifts and natural talents in ministry to bless and edify the body of Christ. Evangelist Tena continues to hunger and thirst after Gods' righteousness and seeks out ways to serve others in the Church and her local Community.

My Testimony

YES!?? What does saying yes wholeheartedly look like to you? Well, I never thought my yes would lead to a lot of pain, rejection, and even loneliness. That is what happened to me when God started dealing with me about my Yes to Him. Now do not get me wrong, God helped me through it all, but there were a lot of rough moments in my life which I felt like I could have done without if you know what I mean? So, I will begin at the beginning. I remember when I was a little girl and I was going through a lot and wanted my dad to be around and protect me from things that a child should not have to go through. You see my dad was in the military, and even though he was not in the military long, he was still not necessarily around much. Let me explain what I mean. My dad was a mamma's boy, and his mom did not like my mom anyway. Do you see where I am going with this right? Let me make one thing clear though, he still loved me. So, he would be in an out of the picture. My mom, on the other hand, was and is today a loving, caring person. She had such a big heart to where if you were down on your luck, she would help pick you up even if that meant staying at our house. Unfortunately, my dad was a different person. He did not want a whole lot of people in our house. I guess you could say that with any man, they love their privacy. During a moment in my life where I needed my daddy the most, he decided that he did not want to be at the house any longer if my mom still had other people there. He gave my mom an ultimatum. She had to put everybody out that did not originally live there, or he was not going to stay there. My mom, being the person that she was and still is today, would not just throw people out in the street. So, he left during a time that was dark for me, thus I experienced my first rejection. I bet you are wondering why I said rejection right? Picture this: your dad who's supposed to be your protector leaves you when you're hurting the most because he doesn't want to stay in a full house and not paying attention to the signs of something being wrong with you. So you're left unprotected to have God knows what done to you because you also have a mother that is working two jobs to make sure all six of her children continue to have a roof over their heads, food to eat, and decent clothes to wear. One thing for sure I thank God for is my mom raising me in church, because believe it or not I started learning who God was to me personally, and I was learning to give Him my Yes.

Some years went by, and I was a teenager around the time that God required another Yes from me. You know when you are in the teen years you say you are a Christian in front of your church family, but when you are in school it is a whole different thing. I still confessed to being a Christian in school as well, but I was doing other things that I know I should not have been doing like cursing or lying. Y'all know what I am talking about. By this time, I have gone through so much, such as being bullied and intimidated by others, and not just in school or kids in my neighborhood, other teenagers in my church would do it as well, which led to walls being built up so I didn't have to deal with it all. So, I was in a Christian club at my school, and we would meet after school. It was good, but I saw things were starting to change. Other people were wanting to add in other religions instead of Christianity alone. One day, God dealt with me in a vision. It was like it was clear as day, so vivid! It was the teacher that was over the club, and another student. They were pulling on me off a truck, and they were yelling at me that I was not a Christian, and of course, I was yelling back that I was. God told me then that I was not fully serving Him as He required. I got myself together quickly, and the good thing was one of my Godmothers came down to run a youth revival at our church. I gave God another Yes and I was not playing. From that point on I was serious about my walk with Christ. That does not mean I did not have my downfalls through it either. Each step in this journey requires a Yes to God. Even so, to where my next Yes was going to require me to go through some more pain and I was only nineteen years old! Did I expect it? NO! Did I care to endure the type of pain I had to go through? Of course Not! Each step may seem hard but remember these words from **Matthew 28:20b KJV** where it says, **"Lo I am with you always, even to** *the end of the age. Amen"* or as it translates SO BE IT! In this time, God was transitioning me from my hometown church where I grew up in and I was involved in everything that I could be allowed to be involved in. At this time, I was choir director, a part of the praise team, I was becoming a junior secretary, and I even taught Youth Sunday School. So, you can just imagine how I was feeling knowing that God told me that it was time for me to transition but knew that it was going to devastate my pastor whom I loved and adored. You know you always want to leave the right way, with your pastor's blessing. I do not care how you look at it. If you are leaving the right way, this is what you want. I was already pre-warned that the meeting that I was going to have was not going to be good, but I still had my hopes up. Well, the pre-warning was correct. I thought I experienced pain, but I never knew that it would be this type of pain. I mustered up the strength to still say through it all that I had to do God's will. I transitioned either way, and God kept me through that.

Are you tired of my Yes moments yet? Do not be, because if you keep reading it will help strengthen you through whatever you think you cannot go through. If you do not think so, listen to my next point. Eventually, I got married to my first husband at the age of twenty-three. He was fourteen years older than me. Imagine that! God sent me someone that I did not prefer to marry. I was young, so I did not want a husband that was married before or even had children. Funny thing, he had both! But God touched my heart to look past what I did not want and gave me what we both needed at the time. He needed me, and I needed him. I did not know at that time that I would not be able to have children. God was preparing me to love the ones that came with the marriage. I did just that! I loved them as if they were my own! I am not going to say that it did not hurt me for not being able to have children, because it did. But God is the God of restoration and comfort. He comforted me through it. But that is not what we are focusing on right now. Sometime in my marriage, my husband was diagnosed with Congestive Heart Failure. We had our few down moments with it, but we had our up moments too. So, here comes my next Yes. At the beginning of 2007, my husband and I decided that we were going to transition to Atlanta, Ga. It was a big step for me since I have never lived in any other state besides my home state of Florida before. I knew I had to go because God was sending me there to help my Godparents who were my pastors in Florida before. He had transitioned them a year and a half before to start another ministry there. Well, we gave God our yes and decided that we would move during the summertime so our daughter could come with us. I had lost my dad that past November, so I wanted to be even closer to my mom too. My mom had moved back to her hometown in South Georgia, which would allow us to only be three hours away from her instead of eight hours away. Little did I know that I would be the only one transitioning to Atlanta, Ga. My husband then passed away that March. This devastated me. We were going on ten years of marriage, and I loved him dearly, but God had other plans for me. He decided that He wanted to take him home to glory to rest in Him, but He wanted me to continue my journey. I did transition, but during this time I experienced so much loneliness in my life. I had to remember those words from Matthew 28:20. I had to remember that He was with me, no matter what I went through, no matter what was thrown my way. I had to trust Him in that!

I made my transition to Atlanta either way, even though I was dealing with grief and not understanding what God had in store for me at this point. I had allowed myself to go into a cave with all the grief and pain I was experiencing Do you know that God will not leave you in a place like that? Remember what He asked Elijah in *1 Kings 19:9*? God asked Elijah what was he doing there? So, sometimes we put ourselves in places that God did not. My next Yes was coming too, and I did not need to be in a place of hiding. Have you ever been to a place or are you still in that place where you went and hid in a cave because it seemed like you were all alone? There it is the word Loneliness. Loneliness will send you into the cave to hide. For God to use me how He needed, He had to pull me out. He blessed me to marry again to my now-husband. Guess what? Here comes my next Yes. This time God is requiring me to transition to Texas. My husband decided that he needed a change financially. This was so hard for me to do! I was good where I was at as far as the ministry and everything else goes. This Yes pulled me out of my comfortability. I had to trust Him wholeheartedly through this move. For one, I was moving away from a ministry that I loved and grew at, and second, I was moving further away from my mom. I did not like either one of those reasons. I was moving to a place where I have never been before at all, and my twin brother lived for years! That still did not get me excited about going. You know how we do; we try to think of reasons why we should not go to where you supposed to go. In my mind, I was even willing to give up my marriage just to stay where I was at. It took my Godmother to tell me that even though she was going to miss me dearly, I had to go be with my husband. It was time to spread my wings and fly on my own, to see even more of what God had in store for me. Scary as it was, I went. Boy, I faced challenges, but I also had some great moments. I was learning as I went. Remember I said that I have never been to Texas, which meant I did not know where I would go to fellowship.

During the five years that I have been in Texas; God has blessed me to be a part of three amazing ministries. The first being New Creation Christian Fellowship, then God transitioned me to The Voice Revival Center. Do not think that these were not Yes moments for me, because they were. I still had to deal with rejection through those transitions as well. Finally, for now, God required another Yes from me. This Yes involved my transition from the second ministry where I was working in ministry diligently, to where I am now. This Yes was going to take my ministry to an even deeper level in Him. I was going to be stretched in ways unimaginable to me at the time. He was going to use these leaders to pull out of me what I thought was dead and re-ignite my passion for things I loved to do in Christ! God required me to transition to The Launch Church SA! Since this move, God has stretched me beyond measures! I now have a talk session called What the Faith! It allows me to encourage others in their faith and help strengthen them through hard times. You can catch it live on our church page every Friday at 4 pm. He has even allowed me to tell you some of my story right here in this book. He has opened so much in me, and I am forever grateful to Him! I pray this blesses you.

KRYSTINA D. COSEY

I DON'T OWN THESE DIRTY GARMET!

Krystina has been a well-known graphics designer throughout the city of San Antonio for many years. She recently found her niche in many other areas after discovering her life's purpose after joining The Launch Church SA. She is a single mother of one amazing son, Josiah. Her passion is helping people no matter what walk of life they have come from She has served in ministry most of her life. Raised by her grandmother and mother, she was nurtured into know God and understanding him. As her passion grew for God, Krystina served as a worship leader at her father's church for a season before moving to Texas. She is an author, and a graphics/digital designer. She is also the graphic designer who a created all the graphics for this project, including the cover to this book you just opened. Her hobbies include the love of nature and exploring God's creation.

My Testimony

The journey to my YES has been that of a unique one. God makes no mistakes; I am confident in knowing that everything I have gone through and experienced has brought me to this point! I had been living uncomfortable for years, afraid to give my Yes because I could not see myself the way that God saw me in HIS eyes. Bondage of the mind is real and prevented me from giving my full Yes. (John 8:36)

I can hear the words repeating in my mind, "God is with you, God is helping you, God is guiding you." I remember my grandmother pouring these words into me and my brother as children every day before we departed for school. I grew up with a pretty solid foundation and a family that knew Christ. My grandmother has always been a spiritual warrior and a great example for me. What always stood out to me was my grandmother's love for Christ and how real and evident He was in her life. His presence fulfilled her. Seeing that I knew that He could be very real in mine. I wanted that same fulfillment.

My scars started back in my childhood. I allowed the things I had experienced as a child, teen, and adult to shape my life. These things had become embedded within me, each experience adding hurt, shame, anger, barriers, and confusion. A recipe for an emotional disaster! I wasn't confident at all of who I was let alone my identity in Christ.

When you do not know who you are in Christ it opens the door to vulnerability. Time and again I fell into the traps of the enemy. I look back now and I'm thankful that God has kept me.

Growing up as a child through my preteens I never felt good enough, pretty enough, or likable. I was always in the shadows, the one that was always overlooked or picked over. I started believing things that my peers said or thought about me. It even occurred with family members. Everything was talked about amongst my family. Mistakes, grades, finances, relationships, everything! I've been constantly picked apart by my physical appearance. Height, weight, athletic capability and build. It seemed like at every gathering it was the only topic that held any sort of depth. What did height, weight, athletic build or capability matter? Did nothing else matter? Academics was another thing my family was big on. If you were failing, you were teased. It made me feel that I had to live up to a certain expectation. The teasing and comparison may have been all in fun but became a stain in my spirit. It's not enough to already have low self-esteem, but to be judged by the very people you are supposed to feel safe and secure with baffled me.

In feeling not good enough or pretty enough as a teen, I just wanted someone, ANYONE, to like me. I became desperate! Anyone that showed interest in me, I ended up falling for. I was easily persuaded into doing things that gave me a bad reputation. I felt that if I didn't do what was asked, I wouldn't be accepted. My longing to be loved or liked lured me into sin. I then just started doing things willingly. I felt that boys only started wanting me because of what they may have heard about me. I had put myself in a position where they would think that I was easy.

I think back to a time when I was home alone. My brother's friend came by looking for him. I answered the door and stated that he wasn't home. This young man took advantage of the fact that I was alone and forced himself into our home. I was terrified. I ran up the stairs as he chased me and locked myself into my mother's room. Her door didn't have a doorknob but he found scissors and got in. My heart was beating fast and a million things were racing in my head. This was unwanted attention. I thought I was about to be a victim of rape! I was pinned down trying to fight for him to get off me. I kept asking him what he was doing as he pressed his face into my neck, his body weighing my body down. I didn't know how far he was going to try and go. I was fearful. I must have had fear in my eyes because he looked at me, loosened his grip on my wrist, got off of me and left.

I blamed myself for everything. I blamed myself for the way I portrayed who I was. My shame grew so much that I stopped coming outside. I would walk to my grandmother's house through the alley to avoid any contact. Some things I did had gotten back to my family. I felt I had disappointed them. By the time I started high school I wasn't considered to be the ugly duckling, I was cute to some. It was a whole new world for me. My freshman year was a breeze, I was happy to be reunited with my friends after having gone to different middle schools. The cycle continued, I was easily pursued by people because they took interest In me (or so I thought...)I was never considered popular, but the little attention I received made me feel pretty and likeable, something I haven't really felt since a child. I dated different guys, but nothing serious and or lasting. It wasn't until my sophomore and junior year that things got complicated for me.

I had begun skipping school, getting terrible grades, and making regrettable decisions. My pre-teen years were replaying right before my eyes. I was more into boys than I was my studies. There was a point where I was just going through the motions, going to school just to be going. My need for male attention during this time was out of control. For whatever reason I could not resist the attention I received. What started as a game of truth or dare ultimately ended up in me losing my virginity. There was absolutely no emotional attachment or emotional aftermath afterwards. Looking back, I realize that there was a deeper need. There was a void that needed to be filled, but sex did nothing but add to the depth of emptiness I felt.

Toward the end of my senior year I had joined a group named Denied Stone. My life felt back on track and I felt close to God. It felt so good to be a part of a worship ministry composed of young people and to be around others that had such a great love and understanding of God. I felt I was a baby Christian and they were far more along in their walk, but these were absolutely the type of peers I wanted to be around. They knew what it was like to be young, saved, and rejected. We would go around to different churches and minister through song. On a couple of occasions as we ministered to different churches I remember being called out by pastors as they spoke prophecies over my life. I came to realize that there was a calling on my life. The things that were said were embedded deep within my spirit and I never forgot them.

At the age of 17 I was driving and had a decent paying job. By 18 I was enrolled at a technical college where I studied office technology. I was at the age where I wanted to do what I wanted when I wanted, but I was still living under my mother's roof. My mother and I bumped heads and I ended up moving out and living with my father. I isolated myself from my family and felt very disconnected from them. When I disconnected from my foundation it seemed like I was lost in the world on my own. I had tried becoming a woman that I wasn't ready nor properly prepared to become.

I felt I had no one to turn to but my boyfriend at the time. He was the most handsome and charming man I had encountered since I started dating. I felt undeserving of someone like him. I began spending less nights at my father's house and more over my boyfriend's house. He had a confidence and cockiness about him that drew you in. For me it was never about the material things or the flashiness he showed off. Behind all this I got the opportunity to know his heart. He would put everyone before himself all the time. He was the type that would give his very last and made sure everybody was straight and taken care of before himself. I adored that about him.

I had never been in a serious relationship before I met him so I fell into a role of what I thought a girlfriend should be. In a way I wanted to take care of him and be there for him as he did others. He was my world and I didn't want to lose him, I needed him in my life, when I felt I had no one. I didn't want to do anything but be under and around him. College became secondary, and I stopped going and never finished.

Skip some years down the road, I ended up losing a job I had due to not meeting my sales goals. I had been feeling weird in my body on top of that, something just felt off. I explained how I was feeling to my mom. She brought home a pregnancy test and wanted me to take it. The thought of being pregnant had not crossed my mind. I was nervous yet excited at the same time. I was indeed pregnant! I couldn't believe what I was seeing on that stick. I was going to have a child of my own. A little me, someone that would love me just as much as I loved them. Someone I could give my all, my focus, and my attention to.

I was somewhat hesitant to tell my son's father because I really didn't know how he would feel. I don't even remember his reaction to me telling him. During my pregnancy we had not been seeing much of each other. We were on and off again. I was back home with my mom during my pregnancy. It allowed me to feel back close with my family. I needed them, I had been missing them. I was able to get my mind right and off the drama. There was another life inside me that I now had to focus on.

After having my son I was going back to church and trying to rebuild myself and strengthen my relationship with God. When I was close to God, I felt complete. I wanted to draw nearer to the healer of my heart for the sake of my son. I didn't want to mother him as a broken or bitter woman. The more my life came together and started to make sense, the more resentment would creep back up and surface. It was an emotional rollercoaster ride. Unfinished business with my son's father would not leave me alone. It seemed like there wasn't a day that we weren't arguing, and the moment we were on a steady course, things always took a turn.

In 2016 my mind was made up that I was going to leave home to move to Texas with my mother. It was very hard

EYES HAVE NOT SEEN – THE TESTIMONIES OF OUR YES

telling my friends and my grandmother. When I got to Texas, life was very different for me. I was able to get back in tune spiritually. I had found a church to get myself plugged into. In attending church regularly, I could feel the pull. I yearned to get closer to God. My mind, body, and soul needed him. I so desperately wanted to be transformed, I wanted to be set free from the hurt, shame and guilt of my past. I wanted to go deeper, because I knew there was a greater love that could set me free. A greater love that had my best interest at heart. I knew God was calling me to come closer to him. I had to tell myself to stop running. From the beginning I wanted to get to know him, but I never consistently took the time to do so.

After changing churches, I became more involved in ministry. I had a level of responsibility I had to maintain inside and outside of church. I had to be a representation of the church. A heavy sense of conviction would come over me when I would backslide. I felt this was God speaking to me. I made promises over and over to myself that I wouldn't keep doing what I was doing to myself, But I couldn't understand why I just kept doing it. It made me so emotional and added so much confusion to my life. It would have me stuck in a headspace a head space I could not get out of. God wanted me to stop letting everybody else in so that he could take his place in my life. The one that formed me, the one that knew me and my needs before anyone else had been knocking at the door of my heart to let him back in. I did not know how to let Him, but he began to minister to my heart and the depths of my soul through worship. Through this journey I found I had a deep love for Worship and it had allowed me to enter a completely new realm in God. God was using the worship to cleanse me. I learned how to worship in my pain and through my pain. As I got closer to God, I could feel the cries, the hurt, and the pain of others through their own outpour. Worship made me naked. It showed me I could be vulnerable in this place and he would still love me. HE would still love me? With my scars, with my pain, with my heartache, with all these things, HE would still love me? I didn't have to hide my scars nor my rejection, I could be naked before him, worship was my safe place. Through worship he continues to cleanse my soul from unrighteousness, from the filth after all...He is the lover of my soul. I found worship to be a relatable space, a space in which I fit in, a place I never have to be ashamed. Worship is an outlet for me. It's through worship that I feel and experience God's presence. In worship I feel completely accessible to Him.

You see my Yes hadn't completely come until I had to write a chapter in this very book and deal with all that I had suppressed and ran from. Bondage, guilt, and shame made me to believe that I owned the garments I had worn all this time. Today I rid myself of them as I continue to let God work on and through me. Today I had a funeral, and the old me died. The life I once knew died! He reset me, he renewed me, he gave me another chance, so I gave him my Yes! He showed me and told me exactly who I was in Him, he showed me a long time ago and that I didn't need to look any further. So, if I look different to you, it's because I am. He's taken me to a New Nation that Eyes Have Not Seen. It's a land of the testimonies of our Yes!

It doesn't matter who you are or where you've come from, the bible says, ALL have sinned and come short of the glory of God, but, we don't have to stay in our SIN; Not when God gave us a way out! Will You give your Complete Yes to God Today? Read the Prayer of Restoration below. King David prayed his prayer after he sinned. - *Pastor Jaundra D. Williams*

A Sinner's Prayer (Psalm 51, King David)

"Have mercy on me, O God, according to Your unfailing love; according to Your great compassion blot out my transgressions. Wash away all my iniquity and cleanse me from my sin. For I know my transgressions, and my sin is always before me. Against You, you only, have I sinned and done what is evil in Your sight, so that You are proved right when You speak and justified when You judge. Surely I have been a sinner from birth, sinful from the time my mother conceived me...Cleanse me with hyssop, and I will be clean; wash me and I will be whiter than snow... Create in me a pure heart, O God, and renew a steadfast spirit within me. Do not cast me from Your presence or take Your Holy Spirit from me. Restore to me the joy of Your salvation and grant me a willing spirit to sustain me. Then will I teach transgressors Your ways, and sinners will turn back to You.

www.ingramcontent.com/pod-product-compliance
Lightning Source LLC
Chambersburg PA
CBHW050736030426
42336CB00012B/1591